ONE MUSICIAN'S WAR

ONE MUSICIAN'S WAR

FROM EGYPT TO ITALY WITH THE RASC, 1941-45

JEAN PERRATON

AMBERLEY

For Claire, Sophie and Jonathan, whose lives would have been more fun had their grandfather lived to share them.

First published 2011

Amberley Publishing
Cirencester Road, Chalford,
Stroud, Gloucestershire GL6 8PE

www.amberleybooks.com

Copyright © Jean Perraton 2011

The right of Jean Perraton to be identified as the Author
of this work has been asserted in accordance with the
Copyrights, Designs and Patents Act 1988.

British Library Cataloguing in Publication Data.
A catalogue record for this book is available from the British Library.

ISBN 978-1-4456-0404-6

Typeset in 10pt on 12pt Sabon.
Typesetting and Origination by Amberley Publishing.
Printed in the UK.

Contents

Figures

Boxes

Maps

Illustrations

Foreword by the Rt Hon. Lord Healey

The Italian campaign has been too much depreciated by historians of the Second World War. Churchill himself described Italy as 'the soft underbelly of Europe', not realising that the mountains made it a bony spine, facing our forces with river after river which were difficult to cross if the Germans chose to defend them. Lady Nancy Astor even described our forces in Italy as 'D-Day dodgers', apparently unaware of the fact that the D-Day landings might not have succeeded if Hitler had not sent large forces into Italy to prevent the allies from reaching central Europe.

In fact, the battles at Cassino and Anzio were as costly as any in the war, severely weakening Hitler's armed services.

I took part in the whole campaign, from the landing in Sicily to Klagenfurt, just across the northern frontier of Italy. I myself was a specialist in Combined Operations – assault landings behind enemy lines – including those at Porto Santa Venere in Calabria and Anzio. Fortunately, like the hero of this book, I was able to enjoy opera in my spare time, particularly at the the Opera San Carlo in Naples. In fact, with my colonel, Jack Donaldson, I persuaded the head of the San Carlo Orchestra, Signore Baroni, to create a chamber quartet to perform for our troops in Naples. Like George Warner in this book, I watched the eruption of Vesuvius in 1944 and had to put up with long delays after the war was over before I could get back to Britain – just in time to take part in the 1945 General Election as Labour candidate for the safe Tory seat of Pudsey and Otley.

Denis Healey
August 2009

Preface and Acknowledgements

In sorting out my mother's affairs, shortly after she died in November 2004, I came across a small battered suitcase full of letters that my father, George, had written to her during his service as a dispatch rider with the Royal Army Service Corps in the Second World War. The letters were in a jumble, faded and tattered, but mostly still legible. I suspect my mother, his 'Dearest Maudie', had read and reread them many times during those years of separation. Although George wrote regularly to her, usually two or three times a week, not all his letters survive. Many of them never arrived, but those that did give us an account of one low-ranking soldier's war. It is an account that is limited, of course, by what the censors would allow, and by his concern to reassure his wife that he was safe and well.

Once overseas George could not reveal where he was, why he was there, or anything else about military matters. After his return home, he would occasionally tell us about some amusing incident but, as a schoolgirl, I never thought to ask him more about those wartime years. So finding the letters, long after his death, presented a puzzle that Hilary, my husband, promptly started to solve by delving into the war diaries. The project grew into a book. The official war diaries of George's unit, the No. 8 Petrol Depot of the RASC, tell us where he was stationed and, although they say little else about the work of the dispatch riders, they do give a picture of what was going on at the petrol depot where he was based. I have also drawn upon other historical and biographical sources to set George's story in the context of the progress of the war, and to illuminate comments in his letters. From time to time he refers to news from home that awakened memories – often long-buried memories – of mine. I have woven some of these recollections into the story to give glimpses of his wife and family and their life back at home.

Although George led the army authorities to believe that he could not read or write, and thus escaped the tedium of an indoor desk job, the letters reveal that he was a competent writer. All I have done, in selecting extracts, is to add a little more punctuation in the interests of clarity. These are not literary letters. George presents no poetical descriptions or profound insights, but he writes in a straightforward, down-to-earth manner, without guile or sentimentality, giving us an insight into a daily regime that is very different from the swashbuckling image of many wartime accounts. George's work as a dispatch rider, mostly far from the front line, was a supportive role that demanded stoicism rather than heroism. Friendship and humour were vital in helping the men endure the discomforts, the boredom, and the separation from their families. He was lucky to have found in Bill Evans, whom he met soon after enlisting, a companion who shared his sense of humour and his love of music, and their close friendship helped to sustain them both throughout the long war.

It was Hilary's enthusiasm that encouraged me to embark on this memoir, and his critical comments and historical knowledge helped me to complete it. I am also grateful to Marjorie and Barrie Selwyn, Bill's daughter and son-in-law, who, after I had tracked them down in South Wales, welcomed us into their home and shared with us their memories and mementos of Bill. But it is Claire, Sophie and Jonathan who inspired me to make a record of their grandfather's war. They missed so much by not knowing him – his practical ingenuity, his love of life, and his sense of fun. I hope this account does a tiny bit to fill that gap in their lives.

Prelude

George Henry Warner was thirty-one years old when war broke out in 1939. He had been born and brought up in the small shoe-manufacturing town of Rushden in Northamptonshire, where his father, Frank, was a cobbler and a skilful maker of shoes to measure. His mother, Annie, worked in the nearby shoe factory before she married Frank and later did cleaning for the taxi driver's wife, who lived across the road. They had three sons: Bob, Dick and George. George was in many respects an ordinary working-class young man, having left school at the school leaving age of fourteen with the same limited horizons and many of the same prejudices as those around him. In one respect, however, George was unusual – he was a fine and largely self-taught violinist. How he came to love classical music and to play the violin so well is one of those mysteries that only began to puzzle his elder daughter when, after his death, it was too late to find out. Although his father had a good voice and loved to sing, no one else in his family played a musical instrument and there was no radio in the home when he was growing up, nor any chance to listen to orchestral concerts in the little town of Rushden.

His other love was the sea. In his twenties this tall, pale, handsome but not very robust young man was working as a shop assistant to a men's clothier in Midhurst, Sussex, near enough to spend his Sundays or bank holidays by the sea. One summer evening in 1930 a young woman walking along the seafront in Eastbourne heard music coming from the darkness of the sea. She went down to investigate. It was low tide, and sitting on a swimming raft on the wet sands were two young men playing their violins in the moonlight. She recognised one of the violinists, Edgar Walton, who explained that they were exploring how the sound of music changed when played over water. Edgar introduced her to the other violinist, George. Finding that she always went for a swim before breakfast, the two young men decided to join her for her early morning dip the following day.

1. George: the pale young shop assistant.

Maud Bartley was six years older than George and a bit older still in experience. After leaving her elementary school at thirteen, encouraged by her former headmaster Frank Ash, she continued to study at night at the local technical college while working as a fishmonger's assistant during the day. With Frank Ash's help she managed to get a scholarship to do a teacher-training course at a college in Surbiton where, although she felt poorly dressed and ill-prepared, she discovered the delight of hitting a hockey ball hard and qualified as a teacher. Maud was short and slim with smooth chestnut hair. Her nose was a little too big and her jaw a bit too square for her to be called pretty, but she had an open and lively face that captured the heart of more than one young man before she met George. She became engaged to one of them, a young architect who shared her enthusiasm for an outdoor life and the poetry that celebrated it. The winter before she came across George playing his violin in the moonlight, her fiancé had caught pneumonia and, when she breezed into the hospital expecting to cheer him up, she found him dead in his bed. It was a cruel blow, but Maud

2. The engaging young woman who stole his heart.

threw herself into rebuilding her life and, as she saw the best in everything and everyone, she soon found happiness again.

Before George and Maud were married, George was knocked off his motorbike and, with a broken leg and a crushed ankle, he was promptly sacked from his job. It made him determined, come what may, never to be at the mercy of an employer again. He was unemployed and still on crutches on their wedding day; he used to joke that she caught him when he could not run away. But, with the savings from Maud's job – she was at that time working as a clerk in a laundry – he bought an insurance 'book', giving him the right to collect the weekly premiums from an existing group of customers as an agent with the Royal London Insurance Society. The business was beginning to build up nicely, enabling them to enjoy some memorable holidays before the war began.

The late 1930s cast a gloom over much of Europe, but Maud was determined to be happy whatever might lie ahead. George soon shared her infectious enthusiasm for the outdoor life. When his leg had recovered he set out on his

BOGNOR REGIS.
- 1932 -

Sunny Snaps.

BOGNOR REGIS

00384

3. George and Maud in
Bognor Regis in 1932.

motorbike, with Maud clinging to his back, to tour Scotland – camping on the way, climbing Ben Nevis, and swimming in the lochs. Another holiday took them to Switzerland, where they walked, climbed and tried to ski. Back in Eastbourne they walked the downs, swam in the sea and explored the coast by canoe at every available moment – not letting the arrival of two children, Jean and Julie, get in the way. They would swim with the baby girls clinging to their backs, and take them on trips in the canoe. On one occasion six-month-old Jean was welcomed by a surprised lighthouse keeper when they paid his lighthouse below Beachy Head a visit by canoe. Maud had awakened a sense of adventure in the pale musician, and her belief that one can find fun and happiness even in adversity must have helped him make the most of the opportunities that came his way during the long years abroad.

1

Stumbling into War

When, on 3 September 1939, Britain reluctantly found itself at war, Eastbourne was regarded as a safe haven. So on the following day, the town received a large influx of evacuees from the London area. By 4 September a total of 7,550 people, many of them unaccompanied children, had to be found temporary homes in the town.[1] George and Maud took in Denis Smith, a lad from the East End of London, and he soon became one of the family. He played with the baby girls and took them for walks in the pram, proudly pretending that they were his sisters. Maud said that she would never forget how glorious the weather was that first weekend in September when the low tides exposed long wet sands, and hundreds of children – whose pale, skinny bodies had never seen the sunshine nor felt the salt water – ran across the sands to splash in the sea, some in their pants, some in vests and some in nothing at all. That warm, welcoming September weather could not last and the following winter was an exceptionally cold one; the milk froze on the doorstep and in the larder. There was little military action to disrupt their lives for the next eight months, but the people of Eastbourne did get a foretaste of things to come. On 20 March 1940, a merchant ship, the SS *Barnhill*, was bombed and set on fire as it sailed past Beachy Head. The burning ship drifted eastwards and came to rest near Langley Point. George and Maud, and their neighbours, donned their oldest clothes and waded out into the oily waters to retrieve tins of food from its cargo. Rusty tins of tomatoes were to add relish to many a wartime meal.

This relatively peaceful but uneasy time, which we now call the Phoney War but was then dubbed the 'Bore War' or 'Funny War', ended in April 1940 when Germany invaded Denmark and Norway.[2] On 14 May a unit of the Local Defence Volunteers was formed in Eastbourne to protect the town from invasion.[3] Pill boxes were built to guard the coast; concrete blocks and barbed-wire barricades were erected to deter tanks and men from landing on the beach; signposts and signboards were removed. Part of the pier's decking was cut away to render it useless to an invading enemy.[4] Early in July a night curfew was imposed on the seafront, and soon after restrictions were imposed on people entering the town and other places within a twenty-mile-wide coastal belt from Sussex to Norfolk.[5]

The evacuees from London had already been uprooted again and sent to safer parts of the country, and now it was the turn of Eastbourne's children to be sent away. As bombs began to fall on the South Coast towns, Maud and her two young daughters went to live with George's parents, Frank and Annie, in Rushden. Soon after they left, a bomb blew the roof off their Eastbourne home. George stayed behind for a while to try to keep the insurance book going.

Fragments of several hurried and undated letters survive from this period. One of them, which appears to have been written in the summer of 1940 soon after Maud left Eastbourne, complained:

> Things are getting a bit thin down here. When I got back they wouldn't let me have any cheese ... and when I went on Monday all I could have was two pennyworth – just enough for half a slice of bread ... I've made a winter salad with cabbage, carrot, apple and beetroot – supposed to be good for you – anyway it's a step towards next winter's diet which will probably be grass ...

Cheese was not officially rationed at this time – it was too scarce to ration – and when it did become rationed in May 1941 the allowance was just 1 oz per person a week.[6] Other foods, however, such as butter, bacon and sugar, were already rationed, and rationing and price controls were to be a blessing for those on low incomes. George, however, was beginning to wonder whether he would be able to continue bringing in any income. In another undated letter, he wrote:

> It's been a hopeless job going round – almost everybody has gone and I'm telling those that are left that I shall have to take another job because my book won't keep me let alone anyone else. I ran into old Dunn who used to live near us and he said some of the agents will have to apply for public assistance and he already knows of one who has done so ...
>
> A 1,000-lb high explosive was dropped in Carlton Road and an incendiary just near our house. I slept like a top last night – nobody to shove me out of the bed – but perhaps I shan't sleep so well tonight! On Sunday night they burst the main water supply to Eastbourne, and we must only use water for drinking and sanitation ...

George had joined the Local Defence Volunteers, which was renamed the Home Guard in July 1940. But in those early days it had not yet been given the training and the weapons to live up to its new and more inspiring name. His letter continued:

> I went along to the Home Guard tonight (Tuesday) and only one fellow turned up. If the regular army is anything like the Home Guard, Hitler will walk straight over.

Hitler had already been walking straight over Northern Europe. On 2 May the ill-equipped British and French forces that had responded to Norway's call for help had been forced to withdraw. Eight days later Hitler invaded France, Belgium, Luxembourg and Holland. Chamberlain's position as prime minister had become untenable after the failure of the Norwegian Campaign and, on 10 May, Churchill was called upon to form a coalition government. His promise to the nation of nothing but 'blood, toil, tears and sweat' was grimly realistic. Within days Holland surrendered to Germany, Brussels fell, and German tanks began advancing towards the channel ports. The British Expeditionary Force, which with the French had gone to help Holland and Belgium, was forced into a spectacular retreat. At the beginning of June, 330,000 men were brought back from Dunkirk to England by British, French, Belgian and Dutch destroyers, supplemented by a miscellaneous collection of pleasure boats, river ferries and fishing smacks. Most of the men of the British Expeditionary Force were saved, as well as many French troops, but they had to leave behind virtually all their guns, tanks and other heavy equipment. The British Army had been thrown out of Europe, Holland and Belgium were under German occupation, and France was left defenceless. On 22 June France concluded an armistice. Russia at this stage in the war was neutral, having signed a non-aggression pact with Germany the previous summer (the Molotov–Ribbentrop Pact), which gave the Russians time to build up their military capacity. The United States was still just a sympathetic onlooker. Thus Britain, with the help of her colonies and dominions, was left to fight Hitler alone.[7]

With the bombs destroying buildings and disrupting services in Eastbourne and his clients leaving the town, what should George do? When conscription was first introduced in 1939 he was, at thirty-one, too old to be called up. In May 1940, however, the Government was empowered to conscript men aged twenty to forty-one for military or industrial work. Not all eligible men were called up immediately and, according to Maud, George volunteered for military service, not from any patriotic fervour but, most reluctantly, from a sense of fair play. He had been profoundly moved by the retreat from Dunkirk and began to feel that he should not be leaving it to the younger men. So, in January

4. William 'Bill' Evans before the war.

1941, he volunteered for service, hoping to join the Navy. Instead, to his dismay, he was assigned to the Royal Army Service Corps and posted to Alfreton in Derbyshire.

A few almost illegible and undated letters survive from this period. One, which must have been written soon after George enlisted, ends:

> They tried to palm me off with an office job this morning, but I told them I couldn't read or write and wriggled out of it.

5. George 'Jack' Warner at Ripley in early 1941.

It appears that the authorities took him at his word – illiteracy was not uncommon in the British Army at that time.[8] Instead, since he had experience of riding a motorbike, they decided he should become a dispatch rider. Bill Evans and Cliff Owens were also picked out as dispatch riders, and the three new soldiers became close friends. In March 1941 George was given three weeks' training as a driver, presumably with Bill and Cliff, and then in April, according to Maud's recollections many years later, transferred to the nearby base at Ripley for three weeks' motorcycle training on the rough roads of the White Peak, where he tried to avoid their hard limestone walls. Dispatch riding was just the job for him; in a letter later that year he wrote:

I'm having a great time now the two permanent staff drivers have both had mishaps and one of my pals and I are doing the whole of the dispatch work – 24 hours on – with a 350cc Enfield bike. I use the bike to go everywhere ... Yesterday I had a run through Clay Cross and Chesterfield on to the Sheffield road to a big petrol depot, and several local runs ... the bike is ever so easy to manage – the gears slip in perfectly and I never have to use the brakes because of the compression ...

Not only was he was enjoying the job, the food was more plentiful than when he left Eastbourne, and the accommodation was improving:

We are issued with beds (a wooden oblong with rope inside for support) and also an extra blanket, which will be cosier than the floor ... Our company had exercises on Sunday in fighting the Home Guard but unfortunately I was on D.R. duty. Cliff was on it and got taken prisoner – however, his captors bought him some beer afterwards – so he didn't mind ...

In another undated letter, written before he left Ripley, George talks about the prospect of a weekend pass and such mundane matters as getting his washing done, but adds:

Could you do anything to repair the case of my ukulele? Perhaps a piece of leather with a strap could be put on the end of it, as I would like it here with the uke music ... I have bought a lock for my kit bag – some fellows would pinch your false teeth if you didn't keep your mouth shut.
   I start my 24-hour duty as billet orderly tonight – it will be an easy job – only have to sweep up the place, light fires and see to the post.

He probably had plenty of time to play the ukulele for, according to a later letter, he spent much of the rest of the year just 'mucking about'. During this period Bill and Cliff were moved to a large mobilisation depot in Halifax – Range Bank Mill – and George, left behind, feared that they would be separated. But then he too was sent to Halifax:

I got to Halifax about an hour and a half before I was due. It was arranged for a car to fetch me there but I managed it to the barracks on my own. The barracks is a mill of colossal size and there are thousands of us here (it is a sort of wholesale warehouse). I was first taken to the company office and then H.Q. stores where they took note of the kit I would need. Then I wandered all over the vast building, five storeys high, longing to find the Alfreton lads. At last I found where they were, but they were out ... I came across a fellow I knew and we had a fish and chip supper together, and then going in the back of the pub for a wee, who should I see but one of my special pals Bill Evans. He took me in the pub and there was Cliff Owens. So now I'm well away. I would go anywhere with them.

He would, indeed, soon be going somewhere with them, but before doing so it appears that the three friends were marking time in nearby Brighouse awaiting their next move. From there he told Maud:

Cliff Owens and another fellow had the job of taking a prisoner to Halifax. He came back late from leave with scabies or something of a similar nature so I was glad that I didn't get the job. Bill Evans the billet orderly uses no end of disinfectant about our place and all the lads in our room are perfectly clean and we keep our bathroom to ourselves ...

When we next hear from George, the three friends are aboard a large troop ship heading for an undisclosed destination. He was able to tell Maud, some years later, that his ship had left Glasgow in a convoy with navy escort, but developed engine trouble and its funnels were giving out so much black smoke that it dropped behind to avoid bringing attention to the rest of the convoy.

His first letter from abroad shows that George was now, officially, Driver G. H. Warner T/244053 of No. 8 Petrol Depot in the Royal Army Service Corps.

15 November 1941

My dearest Maudie, Jean and Julie,

Well darling, I have been on the ship since last ——. We left a port somewhere (the name of which I suppose I cannot tell you) on —— night, and soon after it was difficult to be comfortable in the hammock as our quarters are right in the bow of the ship, and when she pitches and tosses the old hammock swings and dances all over the place. I now sleep on top of a sort of cupboard used for storing hammocks. We soon ran into fairly high seas which have continued since, and in fact seem to get worse. Most of the lads in our quarters have been sea sick, some of them have had it very badly. Bill and I are OK so far but it has been touch and go sometimes. We three are on the Bren gun team for defence against hostile aircraft but so far we have had a very quiet time ...

We are being very well fed. Sometimes we get eggs and bacon for breakfast – I say eggs and bacon – we only get one each, but because some of the lads are unable to eat them it usually leaves two or three each for the rest of us, and so far I belong to the rest of us. We can get all kinds of good things from the canteen – sweets, chocolate, tins of fruit such as pears, apricots, and mixed fruits. Cigarettes can be bought at 1/8 for 50, so please don't try to send me any parcels. I am alright for money also. We are being paid 10/- weekly during the voyage which is more than I am spending. Before we sailed I was well in credit so by the time we land I should have a nice little amount to fall back on.

Tuesday – What a change from yesterday – a calm sea, no sun, but quite warm. We saw two birds this morning, one a seagull and the other looked like a sparrow. Then after a while we sighted land far away in the distance – one day I'll tell you what land it was but I suppose I mustn't in this letter. It was great to see land after so many days at sea ... but now it has faded away, and I suppose we shall have to be content with another long wait.

Wednesday – Today is grand – calm sea, had a perfect sleep last night, and we are having warm sunshine just like midsummer in England. We have had some good fun on deck playing tug o' war, and our depot team beat the rest of the Army, the Air Force and the Navy. It was indeed very hot work though ... The sea is something between a dark blue and purple. If only things were different, I mean if a war was not on, I would indeed wish that you and Jean and Julie were here to enjoy it ...

These are extracts from a long seven-page letter, the first of several hundred that he wrote to his 'Dearest Maudie' while serving overseas. A few words, that might have betrayed a place name, were obliterated by the censor's blue pencil. After this he stuck strictly to the rules and did not mention place names, even in those letters he sent home after the war had ended. He and Maud, however, had previously agreed a code whereby she would know broadly where he was by how he signed himself at the end of the letter.

George was now feeling relatively affluent with 10/- a week and only extras to be paid for. Younger readers may be unfamiliar with old pounds, shillings and pence, when 12 pence made a shilling and 20 shillings a pound. One shilling and eight pence would be written as 1/8 or as 1*s* 8*d*. On decimalisation in 1971, six old pennies (6*d*), which George often refers to as a 'tanner', became 2½ pence.

24 December 1941

We reached a port last week and stayed for five days. We had shore leave on arrival and enjoyed ourselves. The town is clean, modern and quite beautiful. There is a splendid YMCA where we could have as many eggs and bacon, sausages, chips, ice cream and fruit salad that we could eat and the cost usually amounted to less than 1/- each. We had rides on rickshaws which was good fun. One time when we were extra merry we all took turns in pulling the rickshaw ...

They had disembarked in Durban as the ship needed to be repaired. While they were there the owner of a sugar plantation took George and his friends on a sightseeing tour of the town and then back to his home for tea. The family had a baby daughter with the same name as George's baby girl – Julie Ann. Julie Ann's grandmother immediately wrote to Maud to tell her of the meeting and to reassure her that George was looking well. The two families kept in contact, and exchanged letters and cards at Christmas, for several years after the war ended.

George must have left Durban before Christmas for the previous letter was written as he was sailing north up the coast of East Africa. Now he was on a larger ship with the luxury of sleeping in a cabin for just six men and the opportunity to swim in the pool every other day.

27 December 1941
Since we left our last port it has been getting hotter each day especially at night when the portholes have to be closed ... had another swim in the bath this morning ...

They were, of course, heading for Egypt to take part in the struggle for North Africa – its sea ports and the route through the Mediterranean and the Suez Canal. Following the Allies' defeat in Europe, North Africa had become the focus of the fighting.

At the outbreak of war, North Africa and the Middle East had largely been controlled by three colonial powers: France, Italy and Britain. France ruled Morocco, Algeria and Tunisia; Libya was part of the Italian Empire; Egypt was nominally independent but heavily guided by Britain. Further to the east, Iraq, with its vital oil resources, was independent but in special treaty relations with Britain, and Syria was ruled by France under a League of Nations mandate. After France surrendered in June 1940, the French colonies could no longer be regarded as allies. The same month Italy entered the war and although by the end of that year the Italian Army in North Africa had been severely beaten, this prompted the Germans to move in their elite Afrika Corps under a daring and skilful commander, General Erwin Rommel. By the time George arrived in North Africa, Rommel had already begun to reverse the course of the struggle, and reinforcements were needed.

The unit's war diary reveals that the men of the No. 8 Petrol Depot – five officers and eight-four other ranks – disembarked at Port Tewfik (Bûr Taufig) at the southern end of the Suez Canal on 9 January 1942, about two months after leaving Glasgow.[9] While they were stationed in the canal zone awaiting further instructions, George and Bill seized the opportunity to do some sightseeing and they climbed a pyramid and swam in the canal. On 19 January the unit moved on to El Amiriya, about 21 miles west of Alexandria. Here they began the unglamorous but vital job of supplying fuel to the Eighth Army in its North African campaign.

2

Skidding in the Sand

Fuel was going to be crucial in winning the war, as General Wavell had pointed out in 1940:

1. Oil, shipping, air power, sea power are the keys to this war and they are interdependent.

   Air power and naval power cannot function without oil.

   Oil, except in very limited quantities, cannot be brought to its destination without shipping.

   Shipping requires the protection of naval power and air power.

2. We have access to practically all the world's supplies of oil.

   We have most of the shipping.

   We have naval power.

   We have potentially the greatest air power, when fully developed.

   Therefore we are bound to win the war.

3. Germany is very short of oil and has access only to very limited quantities.

   Germany's shipping is practically confined to the Baltic.

   Germany's naval power is small.

   Germany's air power is great, but is a diminishing asset.

   Therefore Germany is bound to lose the war.[1]

Britain's oil supply came largely from the Middle East, and Egypt with the Port of Alexandria and the Suez Canal was vital for ensuring it reached the Allied forces. The petrol depot at El Amiriya, where George, Bill and Clive

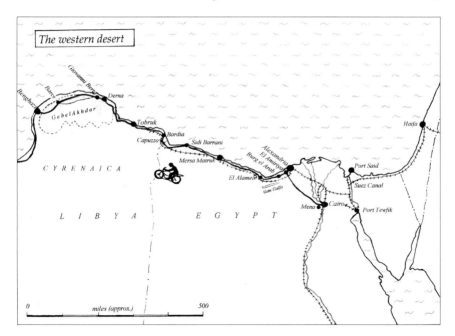

A. The Western Desert.

were now based, was well-placed to fulfil this function, being at the point where the road from Cairo meets the coast road into the desert, and on the railway line running west to Mersa Matruh and east to Cairo, Port Said (now Bûr Saîd) and Haifa. Much of the fuel came in tankers from Abadan and a pipeline was laid from the canal zone to Cairo.[2] Oil was also shipped to Alexandria, some in a shuttle service of small tankers through the Red Sea and the Suez Canal, and some from Haifa, with its terminal for the oil pipeline from the Kirkuk oil refinery. It was then carried by road or rail to El Amiriya, to be unloaded and ready to supply the convoys that would distribute it to the troops.

8 February 1942

We are now settled down and at work and we are in a safe area so you have no need to worry at all. There is little time for anything except work and we don't mind that. We are glad to be doing a job of work instead of mucking about as most of us were at Brighouse. It is quite good fun riding over the rough desert in the daylight but rather tiring at night, but there are no stone walls to bump into out here and I intend to take no silly risks as I want to come back to you as fit or fitter than when I left.

Before the war Baedeker had drawn attention to El Amiriya's 'pretty gardens and a villa of King Fu'ad I' and informed his readers that the 'Beduin market held here on Wednesdays presents an animated scene, when camels, horses, grain, etc. are offered for sale; it is especially interesting in December, January and February when the date caravans arrive from the oasis of Siwa'.[3] The depot, with its large piles of petrol containers, must have been a much less picturesque place. As the commanding officer put it, 'Even officers with POL [Petrol Oil and Lubricants] experience are unable to visualize exactly what some eight million gallons of POL in containers represents and looks like dispersed on and under the ground'.[4]

It was not a place to linger. When off-duty, George and his mates would ignore nearby El Amiriya and head for the cosmopolitan city of Alexandria – Alex – where the attractions were the service canteens, the bars and nightclubs, and a splendid bathing beach nearby.

5 March 1942

I went to a large town the other afternoon, a distance of about 20 miles, with another lad, and had quite a good time. We looked around the shops and had a real good feed in a services canteen and then in the evening found ourselves in a boozer. They had dancing there and also a cabaret show. One girl did a 'can can', a dance with a rather immoral looking style. Others gave exhibitions of dances in Turkish and Spanish styles, and very well too ... [but] the women are a mucky looking lot and look as if they could do with a good scrubbing. The beer is alright but, like everything else, expensive.

Alexandria: the city founded by Alexander the Great in 332 BC to provide the Macedonian–Greek Empire with a link into the rich Nile Valley; where in the third century BC the geographer Eratosthenes, estimated the circumference of the earth with remarkable accuracy; whose port was once guarded by the great lighthouse, one of the seven wonders of the ancient world; and where Cleopatra lived in splendour with Julius Caesar and Mark Anthony. Had George been exposed to Ancient Greek and Ancient Egyptian history at school, and had he had time to wander around the city with a copy of the superb history and guide-book by E. M. Forster, he might, perhaps, have been inspired to explore in search of its illustrious past. But unlike Rome, whose monuments and buildings were to thrill him three years later, Alexandria does not wear its past on its sleeve; rather it survives more subtly in the pattern of its streets and continuity in the way they are used:

Because the city has always been inhabited, people have used old stones for new buildings ... the university has been built where the Mouseion, home of the great Alexandrian library, stood, in the grounds of the royal palace. The market is where the market always was. The main streets, the two that cut the city in half, still follow the line of the streets laid out by Alexander.[5]

Back at the petrol depot, George's letters told of more contemporary matters:

6 March 1942

We have got quite a number of big ants, some about an inch long around our tent. They are, however, supposed to be useful for eating up other insects so we leave them alone ...

   A new battle dress has been issued to me. It is a sample suit of lighter colour and anti-gas stuff in it. Nearly all the rest of the lads wear overalls, and when I have my cheese cutter hat on and a pistol I often get saluted by the natives. The other day I had a salute from a corporal ...

George, Bill and Cliff were, it seems, the only three dispatch riders in the petrol depot and their duties, and their dress, distinguished them from the other soldiers. Their role was to take messages between the unit and Army HQ or the RASC's main depot in the canal zone, and occasionally to provide an escort for

6. Three dispatch riders: George, Cliff and Bill in Egypt, early 1942.

convoys or carry out some reconnaissance work. This gave them a much more varied and interesting life, and more freedom, than their colleagues at the depot keeping accounts or supervising the unloading and loading of petrol.

The task of supplying fuel to the Eighth Army involved more than ensuring an orderly queue at the petrol pumps. At El Amiriya the bulk supplies of oil had to be decanted into cans before being loaded on to lorries to supply the troops in the desert. Huge numbers of cans were needed. In the early stages of the war the commonest containers were reusable, 4-gallon flimsy cans. Later the army adopted the superior German version, duly named a 'jerrican'. Round steel drums, 'americans', were also used (see box). All three types of can figure in the records of the petrol depot. The hard and dirty job of unloading, decanting, moving the containers around, and loading them on to the convoys of lorries as they came in, was done by local Arab labourers. There

I. Flimsies, Jerricans and Americans

Much of the fuel from the petrol depot at El Amiriya was distributed by road in cans or barrels to the troops in the desert. In the early stages of the war the usual type of can was a flimsy, reusable 4-gallon container manufactured in Britain, India and the Middle East. They were cheap to make but tended to leak and let water in. Increasingly the RAF arranged for its fuel to be delivered in barrels, but the army wanted a more portable, and more reliable, container. In August 1941 the army found the answer when it captured 80,000 20-litre steel containers, shaped like suitcases, that the retreating enemy had left behind. These 'jerricans' were easy to handle and fitted neatly into lorries, making them superior to anything developed by the Allies. The war office immediately placed orders for jerricans to be made in Britain and the United States. The third type of container in use was the American small steel drum with a capacity of 5 US gallons (just over 4 imperial gallons) but these 'americans', being round, took up more space.[6] Huge numbers of cans were needed. Despite the superiority of the jerricans, the 4-gallon flimsies remained the commonest form of container during 1942; indeed their production was stepped up as the supply of jerricans and americans fell behind schedule. Thus, when the Allies captured 1½ million jerricans and 500,000 steel barrels after El Alamein, this was seen as 'immensely valuable booty'.[7] The men of the petrol unit found many uses for the empty cans and barrels, and when the combatants left North Africa they were used as water containers – replacing the traditional earthenware vessels – for many years to come.[8]

were as many as 950 labourers on the payroll in March 1942 but the number had dropped to 120 by August.[9]

It was still cold in the desert that March and the troops were plagued with dust storms, but George was adept at finding ways to make life more comfortable for Bill and himself, and the petrol cans and packaging from other supplies came in very useful.

11 March 1942

We are getting quite enough to eat. The other day we had broad beans for dinner. Sometimes we get grapefruit and often oranges and eggs, which are cheap and plentiful. But we don't get bacon ...

22 March 1942

I have made myself a nice bed. The frame is made from wood, and the middle part is of steel bands taken from old packing cases. The result is a nice spring bed. I also made one for Bill ...

Tell little Jean that I am ever so pleased with the lovely calendar that she made and I've got it hanging up on the side of my tent. I would love to have some photos of you and Jean and Julie.

5 April 1942

We do get all the news about world affairs but I don't worry. Everything will turn out alright sooner or later, and I am in a safe area.

George must have been aware that Maud would be worrying about the continuing bad news. Since he and Bill had arrived in Egypt at the beginning of 1942, Rommel had been gaining the upper hand, forcing the Allies to retreat from the gains they had made the previous year. All through the first half of 1942 the German troops continued to advance, while the Allies lost men, ammunition and the lorries that supplied the oil. Nevertheless, George's assurances that he was in a safe area appear to be true. The petrol depot experienced occasional air raids but, despite its large stocks of highly inflammable fuel, suffered little damage.

The unaccompanied journeys that George and Bill made across the desert, however, exposed them to a variety of other dangers. In addition to the natural hazards of inhospitable climate and terrain – dust storms that reduced visibility to nil and caked the eyes, unsurfaced roads that changed without warning from hard rock to soft sand or deep gullies, flash floods that washed away the road – there were the manmade hazards – wires strung across the road, trenches dug as tank traps, land mines, and unexploded grenades. John Saintsbury, one of the officers at the depot in 1942, recalled how the 800-gallon tankers, travelling along the only coast road in convoys of twenty-five vehicles, were an easy target for the enemy.[10] When an attack occurred, shallow slit trenches beside the road afforded some protection for those quick enough to dive into them. George didn't mention such dangers, of course, but talked about his off-duty trips instead:

11 April 1942

A few days ago I was in the better part of the large town and saw some well-kept gardens with lovely flowers including roses, sweet peas, pansies, geraniums and many others. You would have loved to see them. In the sea several people were bathing, and not in the least in a hurry to come out of the water.

22 April 1942

Things are all quiet here – in fact sometimes they seem a bit too quiet. Cliff Owens was sent away just over a week ago. He was very upset at losing his pals. We tried hard to cheer him up before he went. We managed to get off into the town where we had a happy time and finished up with a drop of beer. I got rid of two weeks' money and the others did the same.

George and Bill were lucky; they were still together to support each other through the hard times, and to make the most of the good times. George's letter went on to describe one of the best of times:

The other day Bill and I managed to get off together with another mate of ours whose name is Jack Lord and is in the same tent as us. The day was gloriously hot and we nearly melted whilst waiting for the lorry to pick us up. When we got to town we took a tram along the best part of the beach where there is a little bay and we had a swim. The water was lovely and warm and clear. I stayed in for quite a long time. We had to pay 2 piastres (5*d*) for the use of a little dressing hut and 5 piastres (1/-) for a pair of trunks that were full of holes. (We had forgotten to bring our own.) We didn't bother about a towel because the sun dries you as soon as you are out of the water. I thought of you and our little girls and I would have loved you to have been there to enjoy it.

Five old pence, about two new pence in today's currency, was of course worth much more then. Jean's husband Hilary remembers when, in 1943, the price of a bag of chips doubled from one old penny to two. So the hire of a pair of holey bathing trunks for a shilling was a bit steep. This trip must have been at Stanley Bay, the popular bathing place on the west side of Alexandria, to which George and Bill would return, with their bathing trunks, again and again. Swimming was a passion for both George and Maud, and to be able to enjoy the warm clear waters of the Mediterranean was a great consolation in George's exile among the

7. George, Jack and Bill after their first swim at Stanley Bay.

flies, fleas, sandstorms, and the depressing monotony of the landscape. Music would also be a consolation, but there had been little opportunity so far to listen or play. He was longing to play a fiddle again, and had confessed to Maud that he had been tempted to buy one in Alex but the price had been too high. However, the unit had now applied for some instruments, including a violin for George.

12 May 1942

I went to the pictures the other night and saw the film *Melody of Youth* with Jascha Heifetz playing the fiddle. He plays the Introduction and Rondo Capriccioso by Saint-Saëns and also the finale from the Mendelssohn Violin Concerto. The other week one of our officers lent us his gramophone and some good records including Beethoven's Second Symphony and his Emperor Piano Concerto.

The Western Desert was not, for the most part, a land of graceful curving sand dunes; much of it was flat, with yellow rocks amid patches of sand and grey earth:

You mention the trees breaking into leaf – well there is nothing like that here – no trees, no flowers – nothing but sand and rock except when you come to a village where there is some water – but such places are very few and far between. This is such a dead and barren country that I can't imagine anyone wanting to stay here.

18 May 1942

I've just finished a fairly hard day's work. I've done 17 hours straight off. My bottom is a bit sore from having had such rough treatment from the saddle of my bike. I am on night duty at the office also but I'm hoping for a quiet night ...

3 June 1942

Our biggest nuisances are still the flies and the fleas – the flies in the day and the fleas in the night. We have today spread a thick layer of coarse salt over the floor of our tent and we hope that it will help to keep them away. We have already tried paraffin and flea powder. If you should have any old net curtains you could send them to me. One or two of the lads have some mosquito netting to keep the flies off. There are no mosquitoes here – it is too dry, and the flies and the fleas wouldn't be here were we not here to keep them.

These pests respected neither rank nor nationality. Rommel recorded in his diary: 'Nothing new. The heat's frightful, night time as well as day time. Liquidated four bugs. My bed is now standing in tins filled with water and I hope the nights will be a little more restful from now on. Some of the others are having a bad time with fleas. They've left me alone so far.'[11] Churchill too recalled how in August 1942 he had left the comfort of the ambassador's air-cooled bedroom and study, and gone to the El Alamein positions where he was given 'breakfast in a wire-netted cube, full of flies and important military personages'.[12]

9 June 1942

You ask me if we have any birds here and the answer is they have more sense than that. If we weren't here I don't think there would be any life at all. It would be grand to wake up in the morning and hear the birds singing and to go out again and see the green fields and trees ... We have caught a Chameleon which is something like a small lizard or a tiny dragon. It is a marvellous little thing with a long tongue with which it catches flies by the dozen so it should be a useful pet for us to keep ...

15 June 1942

The sand is blowing in the tent as bad as if 20 rugs were being beaten and the flies are tormenting as usual. After having written two or three words I have to blow the sand off this paper otherwise I can't see what I have written. The best thing we find to cool us down is a cup of tea and I drink a lot of it, but I often feel I would like a pint of good old English mild beer.

I am glad to hear that Jean's stay with her cousin has done her good. I like to think that Jean is with Enid because she is such a nice girl.

Enid, the only daughter of George's eldest brother Bob, was a little older than Jean and wrote dutifully to her soldier uncle. It was a short distance from Rushden to Higham Ferrers where Bob and Elsie Warner and their daughter lived. Jean remembers walking over to their house, past the allotments that her mother tended with Bob, to stay with Enid for a weekend. The house was a modern one, cold and tidy and unwelcoming. It boasted electric light, a fixed bath, and an inside loo. Jean was shown the bathroom with its pale green walls and the clean white bath, but she was not given a chance to use it. Her other cousin Mary's home was more plush and welcoming; it too had a bathroom and an indoor loo with a furry pink mat around it.

Jean's grandparents' house in Rushden, with its small, shabby rooms and flickering gas light, was far cosier than either of her cousins' homes – not the front room, which was cold and gloomy and kept for special occasions such as funerals, but the back room where almost everything else took place. Grandma cooked on the big black range and they ate their meals on top of the Morrison shelter, which took up much of the room and under which they crouched when the air raid sirens sounded. (Morrison shelters were tables with steel tops and wire-mesh sides to protect people against the bombs.) Here, on Friday night – bath night – Jean and Julie were washed in the zinc bath in front of the fire. They loved bath nights. After being bathed in turn, their grandfather, 'Granpy' as they called him, would lift them on to his lap to rub them dry and cuddle them. Then, in the warm firelight, he and the children would sing his favourite Edwardian songs: 'Just a Song at Twilight' and 'I Dreamt that I Dwelt in Marble Halls'. Meanwhile Maud would be writing a letter to George or, despite his protestations, wrapping up yet another parcel of things like soap and clothing that were rationed at home:

20 June 1942

Please don't send any more soap as it is cheap and plentiful out here.

24 June 1942

I am not wanting anything as we can buy all that we need. It would be silly for you to send anything that is scarce and rationed in England when it is here in plenty. I am also well off for money so please do not send me any more ...

I have had a letter from your Mum and Dad and answered it, but it's a job to make a letter up sometimes, as things are going on the same. It is still hot – the flies are still tickling and the fleas are still biting – otherwise we can't grumble. The fleas seem to live in the sand in thousands and jump up on to your legs for a feed. They seem to like me – that's more than I can say about them.

When George wrote about 'thousands' of fleas, he may not have been exaggerating. A more recent writer in North Africa described one ingenious way of freeing himself from a mass attack of fleas. He had been exploring an ancient site near Apollonia in Libya when his five-year-old daughter emerged from a building that must have been recently occupied, with a mere fifty or so fleas on her legs. Having brushed them off he looked down his own trousers and saw that they were black with fleas, hundreds and hundreds of them:

I tried to dust them off. I took off my jacket. There were black cohorts advancing up towards the collar. There was only one thing to be done. I scrambled down the wooded hillside and chose a suitable spot. I started with my jacket, hung it on a branch and brushed it down until I could see no more fleas. I left it there dangling from the tree and moved on to another tree and another, taking one garment off at a time and giving it the same treatment, even my socks, until I stood naked and, so far as I could see, flealess on a flat white rock.[13]

One of the joys of swimming at Alex must have been the chance to escape these pests but, during June, George appears to have been too busy to get to Stanley Bay. His letter of 24 June went on to ask:

Have you started swimming yet? I haven't done any lately – it is not so easy to get to the sea now as it used to be. I guess you would like to swim in our sea which is so warm – but I would rather be swimming off our own little beach even if it did mean getting through the barbed wire. Does little Jean remember it?

One cannot be sure, sometimes, whether memories are original or reconstructions – imagined or re-imagined, edited or enhanced – and for many years Jean was not quite sure whether she really did remember crawling under the barbed wire at Eastbourne to swim. But reading this letter confirmed the memory: the blue sea and sky, the orange-brown pebbles and the dark brown rolls of wire with their sinister spikes that clawed the sky. She had crawled under the wire with her father, and clung to his back as he swam far out to sea. It was probably their last swim together in the early summer of 1940, when she was three years old, just before she left with her mother and sister to live with George's parents in Rushden.

8. Barbed wire defences on the clifftops at Birling Gap near Eastbourne, 28 October 1940. (*Puttnam, IWM H 5103*)

[Undated]

It is still very hot, the sun is overhead at midday, and we have been having more dust the last few days. It gets in our eyes and we get a lot of sandy slime under our eyelids ...

28 June 1942

I suppose the news is making you wonder what is happening out here but it really isn't anything to worry about. We might get a few setbacks this summer but after that I think we shall go right ahead. Anyway I'm not worrying ... I have perfect confidence in the final outcome.

The war in the desert was still going badly for the Allies. The enemy had continued to advance and on 20 June, after a long siege, the key port of Tobruk had fallen. It was a strategic disaster and a humiliating defeat, with 33,000 survivors taken into captivity. But even if George was more shaken and pessimistic than his letters betrayed, it didn't spoil his appetite for fun. His letter continued:

Bill and I had a half day the other afternoon and we went by lorry to the usual large town ... we went skating and had some good fun. We practised dancing on our skates to the music with quite good results and stayed there until past 9 o'clock so that we were skating in the full moonlight. We both wished that our women could have been there to enjoy the fun ...

A few years later his daughters, too, would have enjoyed such an evening. After the war Jean yearned for a pair of roller skates with which to skate along the 3-mile promenade at Eastbourne, but George vetoed the idea lest she should fall and damage her piano-playing hands.

29 June 1942

Just a few lines from your old man to let you know that all is well. I am fit and well and ready and willing to face anything that may be coming – but all is quiet here so far. I was on duty all yesterday and last night and had several journeys during the night but it was grand to be out – nice and cool with a full moon hanging in the sky making it ever so light and easy to get about. In fact I didn't have to use my lights in the desert at all. I am now of course fully at home with desert riding and have got to know when it's alright to go fast and when to go slow.

My bottom has got a bit hardened to the bumps and I managed to get a good grip on the bike with my knees without them getting tired. I guess if you can ride on this old desert you could ride anywhere. If you are riding at speed and don't concentrate on what you are doing, or rather where you are going, you are bound to run into a deep rut or into a bush or big stone or loose sand. I love to get on some loose sand just for fun – you go sliding and skidding all over the place. I am pretty good at keeping in the saddle. In fact I have only come off once and that was when I bumped into two other blokes. I was completely unhurt but I put one of them into hospital. The affair was fortunately witnessed by someone who matters, and the other two fellers were entirely to blame.

30 June 1942

There is not much news to tell you except that things are quiet where we are and that you haven't any need to worry at all. Even the flies don't seem so troublesome ...

Such reassurances can have brought little comfort to Maud as, day by day, she listened to the increasingly dismal news of the war in the desert. By 1 July the German Army had reached El Alamein, only 50 miles from the petrol depot at El Amiriya. It was widely believed, wrote Churchill, that Cairo and Alexandria 'would soon fall to Rommel's flaming sword'.[14] Mussolini had made preparations to fly to Rommel's headquarters to take part in a triumphal entry to those cities, and Churchill was facing a vote of censure in the House of Commons. All George could do was to repeat in each letter that 'things are quiet' and, on 6 July, send a telegram to his wife to say, 'All well and safe. Please don't worry. Love and kisses.'

Although it appears to be true that things were quiet at the petrol depot, the situation there was not looking good. Stocks of petrol were exhausted and supplies were ordered from Palestine, Suez and elsewhere. The heat and the dust storms were taking their toll on the health of the men. The war diary records that, on 13 July, sixteen men were in hospital; a further thirteen were admitted the next day with sore throats and high temperatures.[15] George, as far as we know, remained well; certainly his letters remained upbeat.

11 July 1942

There was ham for breakfast this morning but I was one of the unlucky ones and didn't get any. However, we get plenty to eat – we had supper tonight, and shall have for some considerable time as a reward for the good work we have been doing ...

15 July 1942

It's a bit warm today. They say that we have had temperatures this summer up to 118 in the shade and last summer it reached 123. This is in the desert of course, by the sea it is much cooler. We don't get much chance to get to the sea these days ...

Thank you for sending Germolene which is most useful as the flies go for any little cut, scratch or wound and turn them septic unless kept absolutely clean and covered up. Don't send more though ...

16 July 1942

I have plenty of money having had the first 9 postal orders. I haven't drawn on my credits at all yet. So I have a nice little nest egg for anything I may want later. Please don't send any more otherwise I might get into mischief.

21 July 1942

You mentioned in a previous letter that the old radio had conked out. Why don't you get another one – a good one. I want you to have everything that will bring enjoyment to you. If you get a chance you should sell my bike as it will be a week or two or more before I shall need it again.

The wireless that Jean remembers was a heavy grey object, whose accumulators had to be topped up with acid, around which the family would cluster to make out the news above the crackles. If that was the set that replaced the broken

one, it certainly wasn't a good one – but then Maud could never be persuaded to
spend money on things for herself.

The letter of 21 July goes on to say they had managed to get another trip to
the swimming beach but this time George and Bill must have been completely
exhausted, for they didn't swim.

> Bill and I managed to get off together for a half day when we went to the usual
> large town. First we had a good feed. I had roast chicken, fried tomatoes, and
> plenty of chips, coffee, ice cream and salad ... [then] a lie down on the sand by
> the sea. We didn't swim – felt too lazy for that – in fact we had a little sleep ...

George frequently assures Maud that he is getting plenty to eat fearing perhaps
that, should he complain, she might start sending him food parcels. But the
enthusiasm with which he describes his meals in Alex implies that the regular
fare at the depot was, at best, boring. A poem that Bill sent home to his wife,
with the caption 'From the original benzine scorpions to those poor devils at
home who wish they were overseas', gives a rather different impression of food
and drink at the camp. The first four lines set the scene:

> Hair to our shoulders, beards to our knees,
> Bully and biscuits and over ripe cheese
> Water that's salty, and slimy too,
> Grit in the dixies and sand in the stew.

The long hair and beards must have been poetic licence; in their photos the
men always looked well-shorn, suggesting that Bill, as the depot's barber, was
doing a good job. But, not only did they have to put up with grit in the dix-
ies (large cooking pots), their food was unappetising and water was severely
limited. According to another account, the Eighth Army 'lived on corned beef,
tinned sardines, tinned sausages, biscuits and two quarts of water per day for all
purposes, drinking, washing (themselves and their clothes), and naturally "brewing up". Brewing up, or making tea, was the great blessing of life ...'[16]

Even if the two quarts of water, just over 2¼ litres, was the ration for those
away from the base, it was seriously inadequate. Today, travellers in the Sahara
are advised to drink 10–15 litres of water per day, quite apart from any water they
would need for washing.[17] With water so limited the troops would sometimes wash
themselves in sand, as a result of which 'most of them suffered from desert sores
– scratches which readily festered and never really healed, reinfected all the time
by the swarms of merciless flies that angered and irritated them all day long'.[18]

A later letter admitted that they had been seriously short of water while in
Egypt, but George and Bill found ways of keeping their spirits up:

9. Typical 'Aussie' humour is reflected in this sign erected on the El Alamein road by Australian troops, 14 September 1942. (*Sgt Fox, IWM E 16821*)

27 July 1942

In the early part of the day, when it isn't too hot, I really enjoy myself and I go along singing to myself as I bat along. I do my best to keep happy and a good sing seems to help quite a lot. Old Bill does the same – in fact sometimes I hear him singing away in the distance before I hear his bike. You may think us funny, but we do funny things out here. I suppose we have to otherwise we might go barmy ...

I have had about 12 postal orders and 3 registered letters so I am rolling in wealth – please don't send any more unless I ask you to. Please don't ever send me anything that is rationed or anything that you are short of because we can get almost anything that we need. Chocolate is plentiful out here but it is double the price at home. A bottle of beer works out at about 1/8 but it is good strong stuff and you wouldn't need much of it to get giddy ...

George's letters continued to urge Maud not to send him any more money or parcels. But she, with unstoppable generosity, went on sending him postal orders and anything else that he might find useful, including cigarettes, soap, socks and hankies, regardless of whether they were rationed or expensive.[19]

2 August 1942

Don't bother to send anything for fleas – flea powder is no good – they like it. The only thing is plenty of paraffin or M.B.O. as we call it, and even that doesn't really keep them away. But as the cold nights come they will go away. I'm not looking forward to the winter, though, with the floods and dust storms and the cold nights. I think I shall always prefer being too hot to being too cold.

You say Jean is interested in our chameleon ... [tell her] it had little eyes that bulged out and could look in all directions. One eye could turn one way and the other another. Unfortunately he disappeared from the tent and we have lost him. But we get lots of pretty little lizards that scuttle about the sand and stones. The big ants are also good friends – they are scavengers and go all over our tent hunting for fleas, flies and beetles. Now we are getting mosquitoes but you need not worry – they do not carry malaria out here ...

Bill and I had another half day the other day and we went to the usual place. I swam lazily about for 2 hours, swimming through and over rocks, and I could have stayed in all day. I wished you and the nippers were there.

Please kiss our little darlings for me. Tell Jean and Julie that Dad is making them each a ring from part of a German bomber ...

8 August 1942

It is 12 months nearly since we had leave and for some of the lads a good deal longer than that. It would be nice if we could be moved off into another country where there is life and where things are beautiful and interesting – this desert is too much the same. It might be alright for someone to pop over here for 2 or 3 days just to see what it's like but that would be quite enough. I know I've seen enough of it.

12 August 1942

I wish something would happen to break the monotony ...

16 August 1942

This blooming war is going on too long ... and it looks as if it's going on a bit longer ...

Morale in the Eighth Army was low. Even George could not prevent his low spirits from seeping into his normally upbeat letters, for the war generally, as well as the Western Desert Campaign, was not going well. Although the Japanese attack on Pearl Harbour had brought the United States into the war the previous December, the Germans had been advancing on a wide front into Soviet-held territory and the Soviet Union itself, Singapore had fallen to the Japanese in February 1942, and U-boats 'ravaged American waters almost uncontrolled'.[20]

Now, in North Africa, there seemed little hope of moving forward in the near future. By August 1942 General Auchinleck, the commander-in-chief of the Middle East forces who had also assumed direct command of the Eighth Army, may have lost confidence in the prospect of victory or even of holding back the Axis forces – at least in the immediate future. He had certainly lost the confidence of Churchill. Plans were in place for a further withdrawal of the army if necessary – to the delta or even to Palestine. The petrol depot was ready with plans for retreat and, in anticipation, had listed its stock of 'destructive' materials down to thirteen billhooks, four detonators and twenty-four boxes of lifeboat matches.[21] Churchill, however, was not talking of retreat. At the beginning of August he had flown to Egypt in order to change the top levels of command in the army and stir up some action.

3

PT and Progress

Churchill recalled General Alexander from Burma to become commander-in-chief of the Middle East forces in place of General Auchinleck, and chose General Gott, a respected veteran of the Eighth Army and already on the spot, to take command of the Eighth Army. But Gott died in a plane crash the following day and, instead, Lieutenant-General Montgomery was summoned from Britain with orders to take command on 15 August. Montgomery wasted no time. He assumed command two days early, noting in his memoirs that 'this was disobedience but there was no comeback', and immediately cancelled Auchinleck's orders for a withdrawal to the delta.[1]

Montgomery was in a cheerful mood when he arrived at the Eighth Army's headquarters in the desert and not expecting to find the depressing sight that met him there:

> It was a desolate scene: a few trucks, no mess tents, work done mostly in the open air in the hot sun, flies everywhere. I asked where Auchinleck used to sleep; I was told that he slept on the ground outside his caravan. Tents were forbidden in the Eighth Army; everyone was to be as uncomfortable as possible so that they wouldn't be more comfortable than the men ... No one could have a high morale at the headquarters if we stuck ourselves down in a dismal place like this and lived in such discomfort. We ought to have the headquarters by the sea; where we could work hard, bathe, and be happy.[2]

If tents were banned in the Eighth Army, it would appear that this instruction had not filtered down to the petrol depot where George and Bill had been sleeping in a tent since they arrived. Montgomery was as good as his word, and promptly moved his headquarters to Burg-el-Arab – about 15 miles west of the petrol depot – where his men could swim in the nearby sea. Churchill also enjoyed a swim there a few days later when, after driving through the desert from Cairo with General Alexander, he visited Montgomery's new headquarters:

> After our long drive we all had a delicious bathe. 'All the armies are bathing now at this hour all along the coast,' said Montgomery as we stood in our towels. He waved his arm to the westward. Three hundred yards away about a thousand of our men were disporting themselves on the beach. Although I knew the answer, I asked, 'Why do the War Office go to the expense of sending out white bathing drawers for the troops? Surely this economy should be made'. They were in fact tanned and burned to the darkest brown everywhere except where they wore their short pants.[3]

For his part, Montgomery recalled how anxious he was that day to keep the press away from the prime minister while he was walking down to the sea dressed only in a shirt.[4]

Churchill made this visit to Burg-el-Arab on his way back from Moscow, where he had been arguing with Stalin over plans for a second front. Stalin was anxious for the Allies to mount a second front in France to complement the Russian campaign, whereas Churchill was determined that the British and American forces should concentrate first on a second front in North Africa, to attack 'the soft belly of the crocodile' and make safe the sea route through the Mediterranean to India.[5] But if the Allies were to beat Rommel and attack Hitler through Italy, Montgomery needed to improve morale in the Eighth Army. He had decided views on how this should be done:

> Some think that morale is best when the British soldier is surrounded by NAAFI, clubs, canteens, and so on. I disagree ... The soldier has to be kept active, alert and purposeful all the time. He will do anything you ask of him so long as you arrange he gets his mail from home, the newspapers, and, curiously enough, plenty of tea ... he likes to see the C in C regularly in the forward area, and be spoken to and noticed. He must know that you really care for him and will look after his interests, and that you will give him all the pleasures you can in the midst of his discomforts.[6]

Montgomery was right about the importance of mail from home and plenty of tea – at least as far as George was concerned – and he did get to know his men. He did look after their interests, and they responded as he was sure they would. In later years George always talked of him with respect and admiration but at the time, of course, his letters could not talk about his new general.

16 August 1942

We have got some mice in our tent and nearly always when I go to get something from my boxes one of them jumps out. Several times I've been lying on my bed and watched a little mouse playing – once or twice I have taken aim with my gut but I haven't let fly yet.

Young Jack Lord has gone and I don't suppose we shall see him again until after the war. It is a pity that he should have been split from us because he is only a lad and is now, like Cliff, without a pal. Cliff said that he would give 12 months' money if he could be back with his old mates. I would give all I've got to be back with *my* mate. I guess I wouldn't bother to look after myself much if I hadn't got you. As it is I do everything that will help me keep fit and well and happy for you, and for our little girls 'cos I guess they will still want a Dad after the war and not an old crock. Old Bill is just the same ...

It appears that their young mate, Jack Lord, who doesn't figure much in George's letters, had only been with them for four months, presumably having taken over as the third dispatch rider when Cliff Owen was redeployed in April. Again George and Bill were fortunate to be still together and, paradoxically, the acute sense of what they were missing also helped to sustain them through the discomfort and the boredom of army life.

24 August 1942

Bill and I have got a guitar which we picked up quite cheaply from one of our lads who has gone away. It is a nice instrument and I have quite enjoyed playing on it. I can manage a few of the Hawaiian melodies and other simple tunes and find it much more easy to play than I imagined. As soon as old Bill can master it a bit we can try the uke and the guitar together which should be good fun ...

There is just a possibility that we may be having some leave within the next few weeks. I would like to have another nose around the pyramids. Old Bill and I climbed half way up one at Gizeh near Cairo but I would like to have a look inside and look at other interesting places in that district ...

28 August 1942

We are having a busy time now and have to get up in the morning very early – this morning it was 04.15 and at no time do we finish before 20.00. Still we get a break now and then, so we are OK ... [although] it isn't likely that we shall be having any leave for some time ...

It's no wonder that George was being kept busy, for Montgomery was stirring up action in all quarters. He had made changes to the top command, bringing in men that he knew and trusted, and in his distinctive and informal dress (at first a wide-brimmed bush hat and later a black beret), he set about addressing his troops in a round of morale-boosting meetings. He also introduced training and fitness programmes for all ranks. As he later wrote,

> I am not convinced that our soldiery are really tough and hard. They are sun-burnt and brown, and look very well; but they seldom move anywhere on foot and they have led a static life for many weeks. During the next months, there-fore, it is essential to make our officers and men really fit; ordinary fitness is not enough, they must be made tough and hard.[7]

Montgomery was aware, however, that the most effective way of restoring morale was to engineer an early battle – a successful battle with minimal casu-alties – and this, he decided, should be at Alam Halfa. Brigadier Kippenberger described the change of mood as they prepared for the battle:

> For a long time we had heard little from the army except querulous grumbles that the men should not go about without their shirts on, that staff officers must always wear the appropriate arm-bands, or things of that sort. Now we were told we were going to fight, there was no question of retirement to any reserve positions or anywhere else, and to get ahead with our preparations. To make the intention clear our troop-carrying transport was sent a long way back so that we could not run away if we wanted to.[8]

Alam Halfa was a ridge some 20 miles to the south-east of El Alamein, and about 70 miles from the petrol depot. There, between 31 August and 6 September 1942, the battle that both sides had been preparing for took place. Rommel attacked, as Montgomery expected him to, and was rebuffed just as Montgomery had planned. The victory was a turning point in the desert war.

Again the petrol depot escaped unharmed. The war diary noted that, on 30 August, the night labour gang was increased to 120 and there was an air raid the following day, in which four 250-lb bombs and 300 incendiaries were dropped but caused no damage.[9] There were further raids in the first week of September, but George had to find other things to talk about in his letters.

31 August 1942

We have had some more photos taken. One I am sending is of a little Arabian girl of about the same size as our Jean carrying a petrol tin of water on her head. The women walk about so very upright because they are used to carry-ing everything on their heads and the little girls learn to do likewise very early in life. The Arabian or as we call them 'Wog' women work very hard and do such work as brick making and road mending ...

10. The little water-carrier.

I'm hoping to hear that you had a nice holiday with your Mum and Dad. I guess you could do with some of the sunshine that we get for your picnics up in the fields ... a sight of the English countryside now would be just like Heaven.

For Jean and Julie the countryside of the Cotswolds was their heaven. Earlier that summer Maud had taken the two children to stay with her parents and younger sister in the village of Brockhampton near Cheltenham, presumably travelling along the now-disused railway line that winds across the country from Northamptonshire. Their maternal grandfather and grandmother, Albert and Annie Bartley – together with the Bartleys' youngest daughter Vera and her three young children – had moved to the Cotswolds to escape the bombing in Eastbourne. They lived in a stone cottage with thick walls, smooth stone floors and a large garden. For the children the earth closet – with its big wooden seat at the bottom of the garden – and the daily task of fetching water from the communal pump in the middle of the village added to its charms. They loved the house, the garden and the hilly country around. When they went for picnics they picked watercress from the little spring-fed stream below the village

11. Jean and Julie digging for victory at Brockhampton.

and wild strawberries from the edge of the woods. They dug for victory in the garden, enthusiastically but perhaps not very effectively, and five-year-old Jean, wielding a big stick, felt very grown-up when she was allowed to help the farmer drive his cows in for milking. She knew from then on that she wanted to join the Women's Land Army when she grew up.

4 September 1942

I had been getting your news ever so often until about 10 days ago and then got nothing until today. So I expect some of your mail has been lost. I was beginning to get a bit depressed through not hearing from you but today's postcard has done the trick and now I am quite happy again. If I hear that you have had a particularly nice day out it cheers me up and makes me happy ...

Quite a time ago now I sent a handbag for you and one each for Jean and Julie. Have you received them yet? If not, I will get some more ...

5 September 1942

You tell me that you went to Ditchford and the kiddies went paddling and you had a swim. It has been a long time now since we had the chance of a swim. We can't get away – too busy – our day is from 5 o'clock in the morning to 8.30 at night and I do an all-night duty 1 in 3. Still I am alright and don't mind working as long as I know that you are alright ...

12. Jean and Julie enjoying the river at Ditchford.

13. Granpy and Grandma at Ditchford in the 1930s.

Back in Northamptonshire, a day at Ditchford was the children's favourite summer outing. They would walk over the fields, clutching old paint pots for buckets, to a point where the River Nene flows under a handsome stone bridge. Downstream of the bridge was a little shingly 'beach' and shallow water in which the children would paddle and splash, and near the opposite bank a place where it was deep enough for Maud to swim. This is where George's father also used to swim and had tried, without success, to teach his wife to swim. It was also where George swam before he left home. When Jean was first taken to Ditchford she was dismayed – it seemed such a poor substitute for the sea – but she soon came to love that little stretch of dirty river.

Neither grandparent would accompany them on these outings to Ditchford or on their walks in the country. Nor was it customary in those days for grandparents to take children to play on the swings in the park. They played in the streets outside the house, bouncing a ball against the walls of the shoe factory or stretching a long skipping rope across the road to jump in and out. Even the main roads seldom saw a motor vehicle apart from the occasional army convoy – and then the children knew they must keep well out of the way. Trips with their grandparents were of a more practical nature. Sometimes they would accompany Granpy to the market at Higham Ferrars to buy leather off-cuts for making shoes. In late summer each year, after the wheat had been harvested, they would go with their grandmother and neighbours to glean in the fields. It was a tedious and dusty task, relieved by breaks for cold sweet tea and little white aniseed-flavoured cakes, and for days afterwards ankles would be sore from the razor-sharp ends of the stubble. The gleanings fed the chicken kept by one of Grandma's friends, and resulted in the fresh eggs that, from time to time, made a welcome change from reconstituted dried eggs.

Meanwhile, although it was still summer in the desert, George needed to be thinking about Christmas as parcels took so long to arrive:

14 September 1942

I certainly shan't be home for this coming Xmas but I do hope that something will make it possible for me to get home by the following one, if not before. I sometimes wonder if our Jean and Julie will know me after being away for so long ...

17 September 1942

I have been getting a few little presents for you, Jean and Julie and Mum – I am telling you this because if any of them get lost I will send something similar. Quite a time ago I sent handbags for you, Jean and Julie which you should have got by now. If you don't get them, I will send more. If there is anything that you would particularly like – any of you – would you please let me know ... [but] don't send me anything, because there is nothing that I need and I don't want to have anything more to carry in the event of us moving. In fact if such an event happened I don't think I would bother to carry what I have got ...

28 September 1942

Poor old Bill is in hospital with ear trouble. I have seen him once and I hope to see him again tomorrow. He should, however, be out quite soon. Please don't let his wife know about it.

Bill's wife Thelma lived with her two daughters, Jean and Marjorie, in Mountain Ash near Merthyr Tydfil. Maud and Thelma wrote to each other from time to time, but only a fragment of one letter from Thelma survives among Maud's collection. Almost every letter that George wrote contained news of Bill, and likewise most of the letters that Bill wrote to Thelma mentioned his pal 'Jack'. But although George readily told Maud about Bill's accidents and illnesses, he never confessed to any problems with his own health. Each letter repeats the mantra that he is 'fit and well'. Certainly in his photos he looked well – the epitome of a desert rat and quite unlike the pale musician that Maud met on the sands of Eastbourne. Alan Moorhead, a war correspondent in North Africa at this time, was also struck by the apparent good health and unmilitary appearance of the typical British soldier in the desert:

> He looks at first sight like a rather rakish and dishevelled boy scout, the effect, I suppose, of his bleached khaki shorts and shirt and the paraphernalia of blackened pots and pans and oddments he carries round in his vehicle which is his home. He practically never wears a helmet, and he has a careless loose-limbed way of walking which comes from living on the open plains and which is altogether different from the hill troops weighed down by heavy battledress. The desert is a healthy place especially if you can camp by the sea. These youths were burnt incredibly by the sun and they had that quality of brimming health that made them shout and sing as they went along.[10]

George was about to get a chance to become even more fit and suntanned:

2 October 1942

Well darlings a miracle has happened for I am actually going on leave tomorrow. Unfortunately I can't go with Bill, or rather he can't go with me, but I shall be with several of our other lads so I shan't be lonely. I am going to the seaside ... I think it will be more sensible than wandering around the dingy museums and pyramids and will be the coolest and cleanest place that we could go to ... I guess we shall spend most of the day bathing and taking it easy on the sands and then going to the pictures or pub at night. It's the first leave that we have had since leaving England.

I bet you and the little girls would just love to have been at the little sandy bay where we spent all this morning. I was in and out of the water all the time ... Last night we went to the pictures and saw Spencer Tracy in *Dr. Jekyll and Mr. Hyde* ... Old Bill is coming in for a half-day on Monday.

Yesterday Bill came to see us – he comes each week for treatment to his ear – and he brought me two air graphs and three airmail post cards from you ... I feel fitter, stronger and healthier than I have felt before in my life. I hope my next leave will be in jolly old England though.

Airgraphs, one-page letters from which a miniature photographic negative was made to save weight, were intended to be transported by air. The message was then printed at the destination, ending up about half the size of the original and often difficult to read. However, at this date it seems that mail to North Africa was going by sea. The following February, however, Sir James Grigg, the secretary of state for war, was asked whether he was aware of the distress that this was causing the relatives and friends of men serving in North Africa. He explained that the Post Office could not, for security reasons, know where the recipient was based and therefore could not advise the sender whether or not a letter could be sent by air. Sir James assured the House that preparations were in hand to establish an airgraph service to North Africa.[11]

I am back in the old desert once again after having a quiet and enjoyable 7-day leave. We all stayed in the same place and we had a really good rest. The first night I couldn't sleep because the bed was so soft – but after the first night it was just right. We had a cup of tea in bed each morning and got up about 9 o'clock ... after breakfast we went off to the beach for swimming or just lying on the soft sand. There is no shingle – just sand and rocks. The water is ever so clear and warm and no one seems to be in a hurry to get out of it. I wouldn't mind having a race with you now. I guess this extra practice has made me a better swimmer ...

Maud, who had lived all her life beside the sea, revelled in swimming and was a strong swimmer. She learned to swim at school, at a time when swimming lessons took place in the sea, so she had a head start on George. George, who

14. George and his pals enjoying their leave in Alex.

placed great value on physical fitness, clearly enjoyed the thought of beating her at swimming.

14 October 1942

I think I mentioned that old Bill had been in hospital with ear trouble, well, he is quite alright now ...

We have had some rain and since then we have had quite a few mosquitoes – only little, but they do know how to bite. We don't get any fleas at all now, but there are quite a few bugs about. They are horrible things and make a bit of a mess when you kill them ... It is getting cooler in the evening and in the early mornings, but is still warm in the middle of the day. We haven't had any dust just recently, thank goodness – for that is the worst of our little troubles.

We went to the pictures (which are not far off down the road) last night but it was poor stuff – a silly American film without any sense to it. I would much rather see a good film several times over than one bad one once ...

After having had some rain, wind and dust, the weather during the last two or three days has been glorious – cold and clear in the morning early, and warm during the daytime and lovely moonlit nights – in fact just right for courting, if only one had somebody to court. During the rough weather our happy home – the tent I mean – was blown down and broke some of our gramophone records and slightly damaged some of our modern-type furniture (mostly petrol boxes on stilts). It has been put up again, and pegged down much more strongly so that I doubt if it will be blown over again in a hurry.

Everything is very quiet, in fact too quiet sometimes. And it makes you think that a bit of excitement would make a change.

Could it really have been as quiet as George maintained just two days before the Battle of El Alamein? Even before Alam Halfa, Montgomery had been preparing for a decisive battle, a battle that he decided should take place at El Alamein and begin at night a few days before full moon. George had been lucky to have his sybaritic seven-day leave at the seaside earlier that month, as on 21 October, according to one of Montgomery's senior officers, all leave was stopped.[12] Perhaps that is another instruction that failed to filter through to the petrol depot, for it didn't prevent Bill from going on leave a week later, nor George from going to visit him.

Old Bill has today gone on 7 days' leave and I wish we could have had our leave together – it would have made it much more enjoyable for both of us. Still I suppose we mustn't grumble – we are lucky to have got the leave at all. I expect I shall be going to town to see him tomorrow. We often grumble and call each other the most frightful names but I guess we each understand the other more than anyone else. I think grumbling is a habit in the army – most men are not happy unless they have plenty to grumble about ...

I haven't had the £2 which you say you sent in August and I'm disappointed that you haven't received any of the little things that I have sent to you, Jean, Julie and Mum. I am well off for money and there is absolutely nothing I need (that is always excepting you and our nippers). I am well fixed up for clothing and we are ever so comfortable now. We even have electric light in our tent. I wonder how you are getting on for things that are rationed – nothing is rationed here so if there is anything that you need please let me know and I will try to get it through to you.

3 November 1942

As things are now quiet we have been going through a PT course and are still on it. Together with our long hours of work it is rather hard but I guess I can take it and already feel stronger for it. Through the PT our half days are off, but Bill and I are going to try to get into town tomorrow night. We have one free evening each week.

We are also busy getting ready for Xmas and we have formed a concert party for the occasion. We have got a good piano but unfortunately we haven't got a good pianist. Our special turn is going to be dressed up as cowboys and singing 'Hill Billies'. We already have a lovely stage in our mess hall. Our scenery is good – all hand painted and the background is of an old English Inn called the SELDOM INN. We have good stage lights and also a spot light. We also have a home-made 'mike' made from a telephone. We are dressing up as cowboys with baggy trousers made from tent material covered with little things made from tin. Then we shall wear shirts and coloured handkerchiefs and an Australian hat with the side turned up. Old Bill is going to sing a solo with a bit of harmonising from me and two other blokes, and for other songs I shall accompany him with my uke, and another chap with a mouth organ … then I shall play the guitar with all the other pieces such as 'Clementine', 'Home on the Range', 'Coming Round the Mountain' and 'Riding Home'. We will be around a campfire with red lights and logs – all the rest of the lighting will be out or subdued.

They have promised a fiddle for Xmas – and there is some talk of inviting a few Wrens for the concert. I can't imagine that the lads will see much of them.

While Bill was on leave in Alex, and George's evenings (although presumably not his working hours) were full of their plans for a Christmas show, the Battle of El Alamein was being fought. It had begun on 23 October, just as Montgomery had planned, and a fortnight later, in the early hours of 4 November, the Allies broke through the enemy lines into the open desert behind which they were able to manoeuvre and attack the retreating enemy army. Churchill commented that Alamein differed from all the previous fighting in the desert: 'The front was limited, heavily fortified, and held in strength. There was no flank to turn. A break-through must be made by whoever was stronger and wished to take the offensive.'[13]

Despite the enemy's successive lines of strong points and machine-gun posts, and minefields of a quality and density never known before, Montgomery took the offensive and won. It was the decisive turning point in the desert war, according to Montgomery: 'Rommel's doom was sounded at Alam Halfa … After that, he was smashed at Alamein'.[14]

Or as George put it in his letter of 4 November:

I guess old Jerry's head aches more than ours does ...

Montgomery attributed these victories to high morale and the improvement in fitness that his PT programme had achieved. George was good at physical activities and thrived on the compulsory PT, but was less adept at other daily chores:

6 November 1942

I've got a big tear in my trousers that need the needle and cotton. I've sewn them up once but they busted out again. I'll be jolly glad when my old gel can do a few of those jobs for me.

9 November 1942

We are going to try and form a concert party from our unit. We have a piano and saxophone and they are getting me a fiddle. Then there is Bill with his guitar and we are also getting drums ... The weather has been grand. It is still quite warm in the daytime and most of us still wear cotton shorts ...

12 November 1942

Well darlings the news is good isn't it. We seem to be getting somewhere now and now it seems that I shouldn't be away for so very much longer ...

The good news, coming hard on the heels of the Eighth Army's victory at El Alamein, must have been the beginning of Operation Torch. On 8 November, 100,000 British and American troops landed in Algeria, at many points east and west of Algiers, and also in Morocco near Casablanca. The Allies managed to occupy Algiers and Oran straight away, and two days later Admiral Darlan, on behalf of the Vichy Government, ordered a general ceasefire throughout the French territories in North Africa. Although the Americans had entered the war after the attack on Pearl Harbour in December 1941, they had been reluctant to join the North African campaign, fearing that this would delay the possibility of opening up a second front in Europe. But now that the US Army had joined the battle for North Africa, George felt sure that the Allies would be able to converge and push Rommel into the sea.

In a letter written at this time, George also talked about the recurrent problems of lost mail. Once again he tried to persuade Maud not to send him more parcels or postal orders:

I still haven't received the money that you sent during August and don't suppose that I shall now. Some of the mail has been lost I believe. I am well off for money so please don't send any. I know that you do like to send me something, but I really don't need anything. It begins to look as though the things that I have sent off to you have also been lost.

It was a good job that you didn't send any cigars, which you mentioned in a previous letter, because we can get quite large sized ones for 2 'ackers' (5*d*) each. You would have smiled if you had seen us in the canteen last night. Each one of us had a bottle of beer and a cigar on the go. We looked quite a prosperous crowd.

An acker, an Egyptian piastre, was one hundredth of an Egyptian pound, which, George said, was worth about 5*d* in English money.

22 November 1942

Old Bill by the way was posted as missing in error. So if anything like that should happen about me – don't believe it.

On this occasion Bill had been thrown off his motorbike and taken to a hospital where he was cared for by French nuns who spoke no English. He was suffering from concussion and in this confused state, when asked for his number, gave his motorbike number instead of his personal number. As a result his wife Thelma was notified that he was missing and immediately her allowance was stopped. It was ten days before she received a further curt little letter to say that her husband had been located. Bill's family, like most households at that time, did not have a telephone and, presumably, it was not considered necessary for a private's wife to be spared the agony of waiting for news by sending her a telegram.

29 November 1942

You say that you would very much like to speak to me on the phone like when I was in England. I saw a little advert by the Columbia in which it says that one can make a short recording for sending home. So the next time I get the chance I will find out more about it. I guess the nippers would just love to hear their Dad speaking to them from your old gramophone.

George makes no further reference to the prospect of recording a message to send home; a later letter indicates that he was probably too busy to get into Alex to carry out the project. One driver who did manage to get into town about this time had a quite different purpose in mind. The war diary for 3 December noted that Driver Leather (presumably no friend of George and Bill) was under close arrest for admitting that he had disposed one load of 224 tins of petrol to a Greek civilian in Alexandria.[15]

10 December 1942

Everything goes on the same here – all is quiet, too quiet in fact and I would very much like to see a change of scenery ...

15 December 1942

The weather is grand – no dust and very little rain. We have managed to get some instruments – a saxophone, accordion, and a fiddle. The fiddle unfortunately is only a ¾ size one – a factory-made one something like young Jean's fiddle but not so good.

Things probably really were quiet at the petrol depot for by now the front was a long way away. After El Alamein the Allies made rapid progress, advancing westwards by 1,599 miles during November and December. By 12 November they had driven the enemy out of Egypt. The objective then was to take the Port of Tripoli, which was crucial for getting supplies to the advancing troops in North Africa and for refuelling the British base in Malta. But Montgomery, who had made his headquarters just east of Benghazi, decided that they should take a break there for Christmas:

I decided that the Eighth Army needed a halt during which it could pull itself together and get ready for the final 'jump' to Tripoli. Indeed, officers and men deserved a rest and I was determined they should have it. I ordered that no offensive operations would take place until after Christmas, and we would all spend the day in the happiest way that conditions in the desert allowed. It was very cold. Turkeys, plum puddings, beer, were all ordered up from Egypt and the staff concentrated on ensuring that it all arrived in time: and it did.[16]

Back in Amiriya the war diary noted simply that 'Christmas was celebrated in the best festive manner as circumstances allowed'.[17]

26 December 1942

We have been doing fine – plenty to drink and good things to eat. I couldn't help thinking about you all the time and wondering or trying to imagine what you would be doing – anyway I don't want to spend another Christmas away from you and I don't think I shall either.

8 January 1943

We are stuck in this lousy old dump for weeks without getting much of a break. I've had about one half day in town in two months and no chance of getting in for another for 2 or 3 weeks. We have been here far too long ...

I haven't been getting much news just lately from you but it has also been the same for most of the other lads ... We are having grand weather now – no rain for some days and lots of sunshine. I don't think that is very far off springtime here, the almond trees are beginning to blossom. I have sent off another box of almonds, also some oranges and I hope that you get them. I also sent some money for Jean and Julie ...

George must have known that they would soon be moving, and his pleas to Maud to stop sending parcels were renewed in earnest.

You mention that you are sending cigarettes – well we do get good cigarettes now. We get 50 free issue and can buy another 50. I don't suppose I smoke more than 10 a week, and I keep giving them away to make room in my haversack. I thoroughly enjoyed the cigars you sent and still have one left. Now please I don't want you to send me any more soap, washing or shaving. I've got about 12 months supply. Tooth brushes – I can get good ones from the army for sixpence – writing paper I can get buckshee. I was glad of the hankies you sent and they will last me a long time. Ovaltine tablets – I get good grub now and have never felt fitter, so it would be better to give them to the children. Germolene and bandages – I have plenty and I can always get them from the MO, not that I need them. Now darling, I know that you like to send me things but you don't know what a worry it is to know where to put the stuff. Besides I only really want what I can carry on my back ...

I collected a bit of chocolate for the little girls but at Xmas time some poor little hungry mites came round who wouldn't have had enough to eat let alone any presents so I shared it out among them. Tell them that I am getting some more together in a tin and will send it to them soon.

It was not just wives and mothers who were sending their loved ones cigarettes. The Over-Seas League Tobacco Fund also tried to ensure that the troops did not go without what was then regarded as an essential comfort rather than a health hazard. Thanks to donations from people at home, the League maintained a generous supply of free cigarettes and, by the end of 1943, claimed to have sent 400 million cigarettes to servicemen abroad.[18]

I suppose one of these days we shall be making a move to somewhere. We have been here a year now and I think it is very unlikely that we shall be here for very much longer. So if you should get a big break in receiving my letters – please do not worry – you will know what has happened ...

21 January 1943

Well darlings we shall soon be off. I can't tell you where we are going but I guess it is a good way up. I have been busy tonight getting ready – getting ready however isn't collecting all you want but getting rid of all you possibly can. Bill and I will be sleeping together in a tiny tent just big enough to lie down in ...

Now that the allies were in control of the port of Benghazi, and well on their way to taking over Tripoli, it was at last time for the petrol depot to move nearer the front.

4

Last Race in the Benghazi Handicap

On 23 January 1943 the Allies entered Tripoli. They had now gained control of the three ports – Tobruk, Benghazi and Tripoli – that were vital for getting fuel and other supplies through to the troops as they continued to press westwards. There was no good port between Benghazi and Tripoli, a distance of 675 miles, so the advance to Tripoli had depended on supplies being brought by sea to Benghazi. By the previous December, considerable quantities were being shipped to Benghazi from Egypt and also from the railhead at Tobruk, but earlier in January, severe gales had interrupted the landings at the port. This had created serious problems for the advancing troops westwards, for once the armies and air forces moved they *had* to reach Tripoli before their supplies were exhausted, or retreat. The sea was the only practical way of bringing in the large quantities that were needed, and Tripoli was the next port where they could be delivered.[1]

On the same day that the Allies took over Tripoli, the No. 8 Petrol Depot was ordered to move *en bloc* to Benghazi to take over a site from the No. 3 Petrol Depot. They travelled west along the coastal road, via Mersa Matrah, Bug Bug, Trig Capuzzo, Giovanni-Berta and Barce (now Al Marj) – a distance of nearly 900 miles – reaching Benghazi on 1 February. They would have found a tarmac road as far as Mersa Matrah, which continued in a reasonable condition as far as Sidi Barani, but after that it became an unsurfaced track.[2] Beyond Giovanni-Berta the route took them over the dramatic coastal plateau of the Jebel Akhdar. It was the route that had seen the front move back and forth between Cyrenaica and Egypt so many times that it became known as the Benghazi Handicap.

3 February 1943

Just to let you know that we have arrived at our destination after a long road journey and we are now in a much nicer place near the sea. It seems warmer

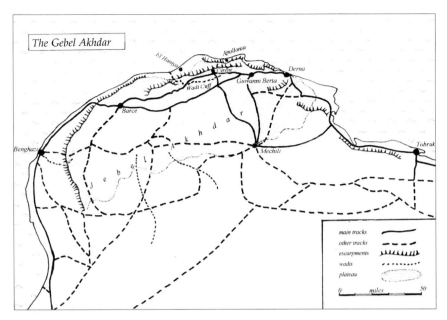

B. The Jebel Akhdar.

here and it will be nice to be where there are trees and grass ... In coming up we passed through a lot of dreary desert, but afterwards came through really nice scenery. It was quite exciting coming through some of the passes in the hills.

We did ourselves very well on the journey, having got in a supply of sausages and tinned fruit and cream. We had some pickles to help down our bully and biscuits. We didn't waste any time on the journey. We were up and on the move by dawn and by the time we had stopped and were pitching our 'bivvies' it was dark.

5 February 1943

We are now settled after our long road journey. Although we had to rough it a bit on the road I quite enjoyed it. Sometimes we slept in our little tents which are meant for two. We had three in ours though for warmth – me, in the middle, Bill, and Jack Kirk. When it was pouring with rain when we pulled up for the night we dumped some of the kit off a lorry and slept all in a heap, seven of us together, which was warm but not very comfortable. Some of the journey we were on the bikes but first Bill's conked out and then Kirks's, and then mine ...

They were now in Cyrenaica, which derived its name from the ancient Greek city of Cyrene, in north-east Libya, and just outside Benghazi (now spelt Banghāzī). Benghazi's roots can also be traced back over 2,500 years to a Greek settlement, and since then it has suffered successive waves of conquest and domination by foreign powers including Romans, Arabs and Turks before the Italian invasion of Libya in 1911. The city remained under the Italian occupation until, after protracted and devastating fighting, the Allies took over in 1942. For more than two years the city had been shelled from the sea and bombed from the air in the struggle for its vital port. It changed hands five times, and each time the retreating troops demolished anything that might help the enemy.[3] By the time George and Bill arrived, it must have looked a sorry mess.

The petrol depot was also in a mess, a state of affairs which the new commanding officer, as usual, blamed on the previous occupants. Major D. Burdett, now in command, was busy issuing pre-emptive orders to get the site cleaned up. One such order, issued on 13 February, announced: 'Attention of all ranks is drawn to the prevailing habit of other unit personnel using any place in the depot as a urinal or latrine; all ranks will check this beastly habit – DON'T FORGET we may have to live here when the others don't.' Two days later, another order instructed them to '*Work* your labour to the utmost. We have a job to do in righting this depot, the labour you have today may be gone tomorrow.'[4]

11 February 1943

You mention that you are sending some music – please don't send any fiddle music, as I haven't got a fiddle now. It had to go back when we moved. Please don't send any more money because goodness knows what I shall do with what I already have. The only things that our canteen seems to have at the moment ... [are] cigarettes and toothpaste. I think I shall start to save a tanner a day in the Post Office Savings scheme.

Well the news from Russia is splendid and I hope they will keep up the good work. It is remarkable the amount of ground that they are recovering and it helps us to think that it may not be such a long war after all ...

The splendid news must have been the conclusion of the Battle of Stalingrad when the German 6th Army finally surrendered to the Russian Army. The North African campaign, so important to Churchill, was, for Hitler, a hindrance to his main ambition to smash the Soviet Union and exterminate 'Jewish-Bolshevism'. In June 1941 he had launched Operation Barbarossa, taking Stalin by surprise and advancing on a 2,000 km front towards Leningrad, Moscow and Kiev. But, as German supply lines became overstretched, the Russians checked the German advance with determined resistance at Leningrad in September 1941, at Moscow later that year, and then at Stalingrad. Stalingrad was a vital target in Hitler's quest to cut off Soviet access to its oilfields and, while Leningrad and Moscow were still under siege, the German Army had attacked the city. The battle

continued from August 1942 to the beginning of February 1943, but on
2 February the Germans admitted defeat. By then half a million Soviet troops
and over 150,000 German and Romanian soldiers had been killed.[5]

This news encouraged George to think the war might soon be over and, in the
meantime, there was the enticing prospect of a swim in the nearby sea:

> It will be a good thing when we get the chance of a swim in the sea which is
> right nearby. I expect it might be a bit chilly just now but I would like to try it.

If George and Bill had been able to explore the coast east of Benghazi, where the
uplands of the Jebel Akhdar meet the sea, they would have found many a superb
swimming spot. They might have revelled in the Blue Lagoon, with its intensely
blue waters and dazzling white sand, or swum across the bay at Apollonia (now
Süsah) looking down through the clear water to the remains of the port that once
served the ancient city of Cyrene. Nor would it have been too chilly for George
at that time of the year. Some years later Charles Sprawson, whose book on literary swimmers has become a cult classic, recalled how his family used to spend
Christmas among the ruins of Cyrene and swim above the remains of its port,
gazing down upon the 'mysterious traces of the outline of ancient streets and col-
onnades, their sanctity disturbed by the regular intrusion of giant rays that flapped
their wings somnolently among the broken columns'.[6] Rommel, too, enjoyed
swimming in these waters – but George and Bill, it seems, never had time to do so.

22 February 1943

> We are still in the same district but have moved into a different camp and I don't
> think much of it as we are living in a smaller tent – Bill and I. We have made it a
> little bigger by building walls of petrol tins filled with sand and planting the tent
> on top, but at the moment it is a bit on the draughty side. However, it will be bet-
> ter when we get time to fix it. There is just room for our beds and nothing else ...

26 February 1943

> Well we are a bit more comfy now having managed to do more to our little
> 'house'. We have dug the floor down about 12 inches and then for the walls
> we have four layers of petrol tins filled with sand and then on top, supported
> by odd bits of super-structure from scrapped wagons, we have the 'bivvy' and
> some bits of black canopy. I have rigged up electric light by using a bulb from
> my bike with a length of flex out to the battery of my bike. So now we have
> quite a decent light for reading and writing. I have got a spring bedstead and
> so has Bill. So we are quite cosy when we get into bed. We have fitted up little
> lockers by cutting open several tins. I always let Bill get up first and straight-
> ened up – then there is more room for me to get mobile.

Last night we had a real treat – the first break since we have been here. We went to a concert in the town nearby. It was an RASC concert party called the 'Waggoners' – all men of course, and they were very good. There were about three on the accordion, two on guitars, piano, drums and bass. Two good singers and one song was 'On with the motley' – which was grand.

It's a hell of a job writing for the blasted mosquitoes are dive-bombing and I have to stop every two or three words to lash out at them. I've got bites all round the back of my neck and on my forehead. Some blokes who are silly enough to go the WC at night get bitten in some very awkward spots. When I am ready for bed I slip off my breeches like greased lightning and am under the blankets so that they don't get much of a chance to have a go at me. I have the blankets right over my head and even then can hear them buzzing around just waiting to have a bite should I decide to stick my nose out ...

I am still riding the same bike – I think – although most of it has been replaced, even the frame, but the tank is still the same. I hope one day they will issue us with a jeep which would be more suitable for this country.

Bill and I have discovered a mobile hot bathing place and we nip along there twice a week for a hot shower on the sly – it is worth it too. The other lads haven't had one since being here ...

8 March 1943

It was grand to get the snaps of you and the nippers at Wymington. I like the one of Julie climbing on the gate but Jean looks ever so sad. It made me think of standing on the wall to see her through the hospital window ...

15. A trip to Wymington near Rushden, probably summer 1942.

Jean, though a serious and rather anxious child, was not on the whole an unhappy one — except when she sensed her mother's unhappiness. But George had unhappy memories of the time when, at nine months old, she had an operation to remove two large clusters of naevi – raised blood vessels – protruding from her back and right arm. George and Maud were not allowed to visit her during the three weeks she was kept in hospital, but each day George would cycle there and climb on the wall outside to catch a glimpse of his baby. He would watch her as she stood up in a cot, supporting herself on its high sides, looking forlorn and abandoned, and he was unable to comfort her. That snap from Wymington can't have cheered him up much, but thinking about Maud usually did.

14 March 1943

I seem to be thinking more and more of you and home as time goes on. Sometimes if I am on a long journey on the bike I can almost imagine that you are on the back and we are exploring again together ...

16. George dreaming of Maud: an airgraph with drawing by Bill.

Well sweetheart we are getting on alright having made our little 'house' more comfortable and we do alright for grub. I get lovely eggs – I swap my fags for them. In the morning after we have collected our breakfast from the cookhouse – which is usually porridge, bacon, sometimes beans, bread and marge, jam or marmalade – we get our Primus stove on the go, which warms up the place, and we cook our bacon a bit more, as it is usually underdone, and then our eggs and then we fry our bread and have a good breakfast. Our stove is also useful for doing our washing. When we were short of water I used to do it in petrol, but now we can get what water we need – within reason of course.

Every other day we have half an hour's PT and I quite enjoy it. After next month I could get out of it, but I shan't as I feel that it does me good.

Montgomery's faith in the efficacy of PT continued to be vindicated as the Allies pressed ever westwards. On 6 March they fought off an attack by Rommel at the Battle of Medenine, in which the enemy lost fifty-two tanks and the Allies lost none. This was a useful step towards the next attack against the heavily defended Mareth Line, over 100 miles west of Tripoli. Rommel had been expecting Montgomery to attack in the night, but when he did, on 26 March, it was in the afternoon. In a combined assault by land and air forces, the Allied forces came in on the left flank with the sun shining into the enemy's eyes and a dust storm blowing into them too. They burst through the German resistance and the battle was won.[7]

18 March 1943

Sorry you haven't been getting much news from me and as I write about three times a week it does seem that quite a bit of my mail doesn't get through ...

It seems from what you tell me that little Jean is quite thrifty as she is saving her money and popping it in the Post Office regularly. Tell her that Dad will know where to come when he wants to borrow a tanner or two. I often think of our enthusiastic little Jean with her shining eyes and our lovable little Julie who was always ready to give me a kiss and who was so upset when I came away.

It has been raining today which makes things pretty horrible on a motorbike, as the roads are really treacherous for two wheels.

Sudden torrential downpours are a feature of desert climates and, although not as uncomfortable as the sandstorms, they made life difficult for the dispatch riders – and not just when they were on the road. It seems that they hadn't thought about heavy rain when they dug out the floor of their tent to make a bit of extra headroom in their tent-house.

19 March 1943

Last night it rained just about as hard as it could and soon after we had got into bed we found about 6 inches of water over the floor of our little house, so we had to get up and fix things ... We were quite lucky as we each have a bed well off the floor and we didn't get wet, although old Joey found his boots and socks floating about.

27 March 1942

I had a postal order inside the AML card. I haven't been drawing any pay for some weeks now. I've got about 15 quid so I don't need it. We have been more fortunate in getting stuff from our canteen and the other day we each had a bottle of Canadian beer, tin of pineapple, bottle of sauce (which helps down the bully beef) and some chocolate and soap. We were short of soap when we first got here, but have plenty now. Don't send any because I shan't need any for a long time now.

I haven't been able to get a swim since being here but I'm still hoping – they seem to think more of footballing than anything when it comes to sport or games ...

George must indeed have been kept very busy if, by this time, he still hadn't managed to get away, officially or unofficially, for a swim in the sea.

1 April 1943

The weather is very pleasant – warm and sunny all day long. The flies are beginning to wake up but there aren't so many mosquitoes about now.

I hear that young Jean is learning to knit – that's good. You might however teach her to darn socks. I'm fed up with the job and hope that when I've finished with the army I'll never have to pick up another needle.

The good weather would have been particularly welcome as George and Bill were making some long journeys on their bikes. George describes one such journey, which must have taken him eastwards through the Jebel Akhdar, the highlands they had driven across when they moved to Benghazi.

2 April 1943

Yesterday I got back from a long trip. I was away for two days and was going all the time – started at dawn and kept on belting along for hour after hour until my old bottom was sore and my arms and legs were getting cramped. I went through some wonderful passes in the hills and saw some lovely views looking down towards the sea ... Sometimes I had a few minutes' break to eat a few dates or a bit of chocolate. I didn't feel a bit lonely because I felt that I had you with me. I passed through some country where there was a lot of long sweet-smelling grass with lots of flowers. I would have liked to have stretched out on it. I did wander a few yards and picked these little flowers – goodness knows what they will look like when you get them.

I went through some wooded country too, but I would have loved to have you on the back when I was going up and down the passes with a cliff on one side and a precipice on the other side, and the 'road' knocked about a bit in parts. It was good fun and fortunately the old bike didn't give any trouble.

The Jebel Akhdar, or Green Mountain, is a high limestone plateau, rising abruptly in two steps from a narrow coastal plain. It is scored by ravines or wadis, dry valleys that are transformed by torrents after heavy rain. The Jebel Akhdar is so-called because of its woods of juniper, mastic, pine, cypresses and wild olive trees. With the highest rainfall in Libya, it is the only region in the country where one can find woods. The cultivated plains supported fields of esparto grass, which was valuable for making high quality paper and bank notes. In spring the fields would have been bursting briefly into bloom, with 'pink and yellow sage, yellow camel-thorn, white and pink anemones, purple gladioli, pink convolvulus, red poppies, and other small rainbow-hued blossoms by the score'.[8]

Bill was also making long, tiring trips on his bike, and one of his trips ended rather uncomfortably:

Poor old Bill came back from a long trip when he ran into someone – got a broken nose, two lovely black eyes and a cut on his head. He is OK now though and out of hospital. Don't tell his Missus in case he hasn't told her.

The other unfortunate victim of this accident was a local man. Bill was not held responsible; indeed he was told, 'You should have killed the bugger.'[9]

10 April 1943

Well darling, last night I got back from a 500-mile trip and was away for two days and everything went well. The road was a bit greasy for the start but after about 10 miles it dried up and gave me a chance to get moving better. On the wet roads I cut my speed down to half and out here you have to be always on the look out for potholes – also wild dogs that go about in small packs – sometimes they fetch a camel down and eat his tummy out. I always have my 'gut' loaded up and plenty of spare slugs, but when I see them about I never stop ... On this trip I passed the best scenery, including mountain passes and a wonderful gorge, with rocks towering up on either side and a number of great caverns, and the road winding up and down and from side to side like a scenic railway ...

This trip must again have taken him over the Jebel Akhdar, for the Jebel is the only highland region within 250 miles of Benghazi. On this journey he appears to have driven along the more northerly road which took him across the Wadi Kuf – the Valley of the Caves – a spectacular deep wadi that cuts through this upland, with sheer cliffs, deep caves, stony crags and thickly wooded hillsides. He would have crossed the wadi at its deepest point by two Bailey bridges, built by the Royal Engineers after the Italians had blown up the concrete bridges on their retreat westwards.[10]

While George and Bill were making these journeys, perhaps to take messages to contacts in the east in preparation for the withdrawal to Suez, the front line of the Eighth Army was making progress nearly 1,000 miles to the west of Benghazi, across some of the roughest and most inhospitable terrain on earth. On 8 April, having broken through the Mareth Line (a line of old French fortifications beyond the Wadi Zigzaou) and then through the Gabes Gap, they met up with the Allies, who had landed further west as part of Operation Torch (see map on page 75).

15 April 1943

Everything is going on well and I suppose the present campaign here will soon be over. I wonder what will happen next – anyhow I feel a good deal nearer to you than a few months ago ...

By now, with victory in North Africa nearly assured, plans were in place for the next move, codenamed Operation Husky: the invasion of Sicily. At their conference in Casablanca the previous January, Churchill and Roosevelt had agreed to mount an attack on Sicily on two fronts, with Eisenhower as supreme commander and Alexander as deputy commander-in-chief. General Patton would head a 'western task force' and Montgomery would be in charge of an 'eastern task force'. But there had been much disagreement about tactics. Montgomery, who believed in concentrating his attacks, had argued that the forces should land on a narrower beach-front than was originally proposed. Montgomery got his way.[11] The Eighth Army would remain as a single fighting force, and would land at Sicily in the concentrated formation that he favoured.

21 April 1943

The warm weather has come now and we have change into our KD clothing ... Haven't done any swimming this year yet, but hope to before long.

22 April 1943

Yesterday I got back from another long trip, having been away for two days. We get these trips in turn about once a week. They make a change but it is a bit tiring riding for hours, sometimes with the road bunged up with traffic and sometimes going about 100 miles without seeing a soul.

Back at base, life posed different challenges:

29 April 1943

I've just come in from chasing two asps – one got away but I killed the other with an iron bar. They are nasty things, half way between a lizard and a snake, and I think the poison comes out through a hole in their teeth. The 'Wogs' say one bite from them, and 'finish'. There are quite a lot of them about now.

9 May 1943

Bill and I were invited to a party and we went there last night. We had to take something else to town so it was partly official and we went on one motorbike. When we got there we went into the lads' quarters where we got the dust from the roads off, washed ourselves and polished our boots and then in we went to meet the ladies. We had a few vermouths first to give us a bit of courage – to some people you know the idea of asking a young lady for a dance is far more terrifying than a few bombs – but I was soon happy enough with a sweet young kid ... [she] was about sixteen but somehow she reminded me of our Jean. I think we both were a bit nervous or awkward to start and we both kept apologising to each other, but soon we were doing fine and when the vermouth started to work I was trying out new steps ... I'm going to try hard to be able to dance so that I can take my missus and kids out when I get back – for I know that is something you like and I haven't done much for you in the past ...

From your ever-loving – yes, and faithful – husband.

In a letter to Jean, George wrote that his young dancing partner was a school-girl called Anna, presumably from the local Italian community. Maud loved to dance, preferring the energetic country dances to the more sophisticated fox-trots and quicksteps of the day, but George was a bit of a novice when it came to dancing. Nor was he likely to get any more practice in the near future for, two days before this letter was written, a patrol of US II Corps met up with one from the 4th Indian Division so that 'the two armies which had started two thousand miles apart, were now at last joined together'.[12] On 13 May Alexander signalled to Churchill, 'It is my duty to report that the Tunisian Campaign is over. All enemy resistance has ceased. We are masters of the North African shores.'[13]

On the day that George was polishing his boots and downing a few vermouths to give him courage to ask a young girl to dance, the petrol depot was ordered to move back to the Suez area. Three days later, George and Bill were on the road, retracing the route they had taken four months earlier, over the Jebel Akhdar and through the Derna Pass, to Bardia, Mersa Matruh, and El Amiriya, but this time they continued on for another 192 miles via Mena, just outside Cairo, to an RASC mobilisation centre in the canal area where they would await their next move.[14]

Two days after reaching the mobilisation centre, on 19 May, the Axis forces capitulated. The war in Africa was now officially over and the invasion of Sicily could go ahead. The rest of the Eighth Army forces were brought back to the Suez–Alexandria region ready to set sail for Sicily.[15] They would need to travel lightly. When George and Bill left El Amiriya, most of their possessions had been thrown away or left to be forwarded later, and once again they would have to throw things out – but could Maud be dissuaded from sending him more parcels?

24 May 1943

I am ever so fit and well and have everything that I need. Please *don't* send me any money or anything except your news ... if you don't get much news from me, don't worry – I shall be all right.

26 May 1943

I have had several rolls of music but I am afraid it isn't any use to me now, so I am sending the good stuff back. Please don't send any more as I have far too much stuff already.

7 June 1943

Here is five quid which I would like you to use for buying something nice when you go on picnics ... I still have more than enough money, more than I know what to do with so please *don't* send me any more ...

We go bathing in the sea everyday now. It has been quite rough and it has been grand fun jumping over the rollers.

21 June 1943

I am glad that you got the sugar and coffee from the Victoria League South Africa ... I didn't mention it in case it never reached you ... and that you are getting oranges through now. We get plenty of them and I am never tired of eating them ... [but] please *don't* send me anything except your letters ...

26 June 1943

Many thanks for the registered parcel containing braces from Jean, tooth brush from Julie and a pen from you, which I think was meant for my birthday. Although it arrived a bit late, it was jolly nice to have ... [but] please *don't* send anything else until I let you know. The other week I sent off a necklace to match your brooch and bracelet – something like the one that got lost. I do hope you get this one.

On 19 June George sent a telegram to Maud assuring her that all was well, and the short letters that followed continued to urge her not to send him money or parcels, an exhortation she continued to ignore. During their stay in the desert the mail between Egypt and England was frequently delayed or lost, and letters between George and Maud would sometimes take two months to arrive. As for the birthday presents that he received on 26 June, Maud would have posted these well before his birthday on 18 April, so that parcel must have taken even longer. And one wonders how drinkable the coffee that George sent Maud from South Africa was. It arrived nearly a year and a half after it was posted.

27 June 1943

We saw a film last evening called *Love Crazy*. It was an open air show and we all sat on the sand ... Just come back from a swim and the water was ever so warm. We go every day now and it is quite enjoyable except that it is a long tramp through the soft sand ...

The sandy beaches all along the coast were thronged with troops, all making the most of their last days in North Africa. Some must have been anxious about what was in store for them, others were eager to move on. Much as he loved to swim, George was only too glad to leave the desert and move a little closer towards victory and home. But what of those for whom the desert was home – the soldiers in the Libyan Arab Force who had fought alongside the British, the Egyptian labourers who had loaded and unloaded fuel, and the young girls who carried water on their heads to the troops? A dozen years later an American diplomat to the newly independent Libya described the mess they left behind on the coast road between Benghazi and Alexandria:

For endless miles it is littered with the carcasses of tanks, trunks, and buses – stripped by the nomads to the last bolt, corroding in the wind and the weather. Goats and camels forage among gasoline drums, the bare skeletons of planes, tin cans and heaps of scrap. It is no wonder that the wealth of Cyrenaica is said to lie in its scrap iron. Even the demolished city of Tobruk ... was a relief after viewing the shaky huts of tin ranged alongside the Bedouin tens by the side of the road.[16]

Off the road, and less visible, lurked the land mines – many of which are still there, killing or maiming unsuspecting shepherds or children playing in the desert sands. Such concerns, however, were probably far from the thoughts of George and his mates from the petrol depot. On 30 June, they boarded their troop ship ready to take part in the Allied invasion of Sicily. Along with their weapons, vehicles and equipment, the two canny dispatch riders, George and Bill, made sure they found room for their gramophone, records and a Primus stove.

5

An Orchard in Sunny Sicily

Only the greatest folly could lead one to contemplate an invasion. No one will ever land here, not even a single soldier![1]

Thus boasted Benito Mussolini in 1937 of Sicily's preparedness on land, at sea, and in the air. Six years later the largest seaborne invasion that had ever been mounted – 2,590 vessels carrying 180,000 troops – converged on the southern shores of Sicily. 1,614 British and 945 American ships took part in Operation Husky, the remainder being Belgian, Dutch, Greek, Norwegian and Polish. Most of them had sailed from the Eastern Mediterranean – from Suez, Port Said, Alexandria, Haifa and Beirut – with others coming from the west, from ports in Algeria and Tunisia and even as far away as the Clyde. George and Bill were now aboard the SS *Orbita*, which in its happier days had been a passenger ship of the Royal Mail Lines and later was to have its own footnote in history when, in 1948, it sailed to Britain with 100 Caribbean immigrants alongside the more renowned *Empire Woodrush*, with its 400 passengers. The invading fleet moved slowly westwards, hugging the north coast of Africa, to meet up with the US 7th Army 50 miles south of Sicily at noon on 9 July, ready for the combined assault the following day.

The plan that had eventually been adopted was for the British forces, under Montgomery, to land in two main bodies on a stretch of coast to the south-east of the island, between Syracuse and Pozzallo. The Americans, under Patton, would land on the south-west coast, mainly between Cap Scaramia and Licata. Operation Mincemeat had tricked the Germans into believing that the Allies would mount their main attacks in Greece and Sardinia, with only a subsidiary assault on Sicily, and the German forces on the island had been drastically reduced. General Guzzoni, who had been pulled out of retirement by Mussolini

II. Translation of Two Leaflets Bill Sent Home to Thelma

WHY DIE FOR HITLER?

You, Italian soldiers, have no interest in fighting this war. Like the millions of Italian men, women and children, i.e. Italy, who have everything to lose if this war continues.

This is Hitler's war.

No one has provoked Italy; no one has attacked Italy; no one has declared war on Italy.

Hitler himself is making Italy a shield against the crushing superiority of the United Nations, as the bulletins of the Axis acknowledge. This means death, ruin and grief for Italians.

Yesterday Hitler condemned and sacrificed Italians in Africa. Today he sacrifices Italians in Italy.

Germany will fight to the end ... the end of Italy.

Nobody asked you whether you want this war. But they have sent you to die. They have told you: 'BELIEVE, OBEY, FIGHT.'

Why? For whom? For what?

Why die for Hitler?

WARNING!

Defeated soldiers of Tunis, now you are back, if you side with the Germans, you put yourself on the battlefield of Germany's southern front.

The conquest of Tunisia releases the Anglo–American air force and leaves them free to attack military targets in Italy. This means that all the installations, the arsenals, the ports, the railways, the bridges and the roads of Italy, are bound to experience air raids, night and day. All those who continue to live close to military targets inevitably risk being killed or wounded.

You must thank Mussolini and his master Hitler. Remember Mussolini's speech of 18 November 1940: 'I have asked for, and secured, the Fuhrer's agreement for our planes to participate directly in the battle against Great Britain...'

Time for Italy to go into mourning.

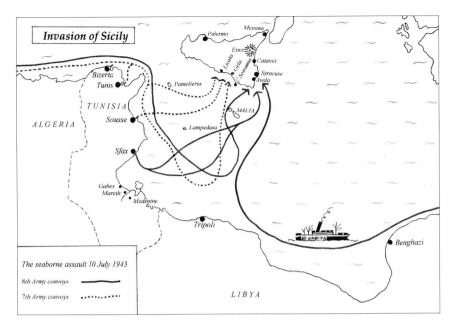

C. The Invasion of Sicily.

to command the army in Sicily two months before, found that the beaches were generally undefended, adding that 'a number of blockhouses and fortifications had been built, but most of them were unmanned. On the highway from Licata to Campobello, for example, a distance of 12 miles, the whole antitank defence was one 470-mm gun.'[2] A British intelligence officer was greatly encouraged when aerial reconnaissance photographs showed women bathing on the beach he was to attack.[3]

Before the invasion the Allies had dropped leaflets urging the Italian forces not to resist, but it was the weather, rather than the enemy, that hampered the landings. As the two British divisions headed for Avola in the bay south of Syracuse, a force-six wind blew up. Waves swamped the boats; many last suppers were added to the bilge water as the men struggled to bale out; the spray rendered binoculars useless; compass lights fused and many wireless sets went dead; the wind blew the vessels off course; the landings were chaotic.[4] But, according to the official history, 'by a little after 6 a.m. all troops were ashore; the warships at intervals beat down some wavering enemy guns; and 151st Brigade quickly and steadily mopped up, and moved on to its prescribed positions west of Avola'.[5]

It was not until ten days later, on 20 July, that George could send Maud a telegram urging her not to worry. Soon after, his letters began again.

24 July 1943

At last I am able to write and let you know that all is going on OK. I am fit and well, although we now seem to be working practically all the time. I shall have a lot to tell you when I come home but of course I can't tell you much now. I have the feeling that it won't be so very long before we meet again anyway.

The petrol depot was now established in Targia, some 4 miles north-west of Syracuse and outside the walls of Dionysius, which had once stretched about 12 miles around the largest and most heavily fortified ancient Greek city – a city that had long since shrunk back to become a small town clustered around its sheltering harbour. Situated on the railway line to Catania in the north and the port of Syracuse to the south, the depot was serving all the Allied forces on the island except the Americans, and the men were working flat-out to meet the demands upon them. An entry in the war diary for 24 July reads: '200 tons train arrived last light for sorting, re-loading and off-loading and ready for pulling out at 0630 hours 25th July. This is fourth 24-hour period continuously worked by *whole* unit – all ranks.'[6]

17. Postcard from Syracuse: part of the walls of Dionysus.

Although George and Bill were having to work hard, it seems that once again they found themselves in a relatively safe place that was soon well behind the front. The two armies were pressing northwards, inch by inch, with Mongomery leading the attack up the eastern coast towards Catania, and Patton taking the inland route toward Palermo, both anxious to be the first to reach Messina. By 17 July the Eighth Army had at last secured the Primsole Bridge, on the road to Catania, after several days of battle that left hundreds dead and wounded. In contrast, the depot suffered little from enemy attack; the war diary mentions only one air raid while it was in Sicily and this appears to have done no significant damage. The entries note only minor incidents, some caused by the enemy and some by the Allies. On 17 July fires were started by some Allied forces, who, according to the war diaries, had 'no idea of dispersal and march discipline'. In a rare reference to the enemy, orders were given on 24 July to apprehend the owner of a farm near the depot. He was suspected of Fascist leanings. The next day 'Bren Gun fire eliminated the nuisance' of sniping behind the depot.[7] This is the only reference to hostile action made by men at the depot over the whole campaign.

George paints a peaceful, bucolic picture of his new home in an orchard by the sea, presumably a little way away from the petrol depot:

30 July 1943

We are getting plenty to eat. We can have as many lemons, tomatoes, almond nuts, pears as we like – they only need picking up. We can also get wine but no beer. I had a swim in the sea the other night and thoroughly enjoyed it ... I wish you could swim in the lovely blue sea near here – you would just love it.

George's letters were now headed 'Central Mediterranean Forces' instead of 'Middle Eastern Forces':

7 August 1943

You will see that my official address is at last altered. Everything is going on fine now and all is quite quiet and safe and I am fit and well and enjoying life more now than for quite a time. We have pitched our tent – that is Bill, Joey and myself – in an orchard of lemon, orange and almond trees ... We only use our tents to keep our little bit of kit in and we sleep in the open with just a sheet of canvas stretched overhead. We do use the mosquito nets just in case.

There are quite a lot of grapes about now, also pears including prickly pears, and other fruits, and in our orchard there are lemons and nuts. The oranges aren't quite ready yet. We are getting more food than we need and there is plenty of water which usually we draw from wells. We had another swim last evening and the sea is grand – warm, clear and calm, just right for swimming. I would like to have the old canoe here to explore the coast.

It was lucky for George and Bill that they arrived in the summer and among fields of ripe tomatoes and orchards laden with fruit for, according to Maud, they had landed with only 48 hours of rations and had to scavenge for themselves. In fact, apart from the separation from their families, they could hardly have found themselves in a pleasanter spot and at a better time of the year. General Ridgway commented:

> No war was ever fought, I think, in more ideal weather than the Sicilian campaign. The soft spring lay upon the land like a benediction; the days were warm, the nights cool, and there was no rain. After the frying pan of Africa, the balmy weather was like heaven to the troopers who had suffered through Morocco and Tunisia. There were no insects, except mosquitoes, and these were no problem.[8]

Had the American general been living in a tent in an orchard, he would have noticed the flies and the ants. Nor was Sicily easy country for those nearer the front. Brigadier Molony, in the official history, describes the difficult terrain and conditions that confronted the invading forces as 'rocky mountains and hills, pierced by narrow, enclosed valleys and dry watercourses ... the climate is like that of North Africa and in July a usual day-temperature is 75° Fahrenheit or a few degrees above ... there is no rain to cool the earth or lay the dust ... Malaria and sandfly fever are ubiquitous enemies.'[9] Molony concludes that it was a country where the advantages lie almost wholly with those defending it.

However, having survived the confusion, discomfort and terror of their landing, George, Bill and Joey were finding life in Sicily a welcome change from the desert:

> *9 August 1943*
>
> I am having quite an easy time now – it has been a bit hard up to now – but it has been worth it especially to get away from the beastly sand ... also life seems more interesting ... We now get the chance of a short swim almost every day in the lovely calm blue sea. There are no sands, but mostly a sort of volcanic rock from which we either dive or wade.
>
> We managed to smuggle our old Primus stove and it is jolly handy when we want a brew up or do a bit of cooking. There are lots of flies about which are a nuisance – also a lot of lizards and ants. The ants crawl all over us but they don't seem to bite. We killed an asp but that is the only one I have seen so far.
>
> I want to send you some lemons and almond nuts but so far haven't been able to get hold of a box. Anyway I'll try and rig something up. I can only send 2 lbs – there is enough in this orchard to send 2 tons.
>
> There are some lovely kiddies here and all the lads are good to them and give them chocolate and biscuits. It is a real treat to watch their faces and see

18. Children playing in a badly bombed street in Sicily, 1943. *(Lt Chetwyn, IWM TR 1240)*

the nice way in which they thank you. I always feel that whoever started this blinking war, they certainly didn't.

12 August 1943

I bet you have guessed by now that I am in 'Sunny Sicily' and it is true enough the sun shines all day long ... [and] I am getting nearer home now – there is only about 23 miles of sea between us ...

He was, indeed, nearer to home, and not just in terms of distance. He had left the desert, whose barrenness appalled him, and a culture of which he had little knowledge, for a fertile land whose people shared the musical tradition that meant so much to him.

While George was making himself comfortable with Bill and Joey in the orchard, there was a change of command at the depot and, as usual, the new commanding officer was scornful of the way his predecessor had been managing the site. The war diary for 15 August notes the 'complete chaos reigning in this unit through orders given by the previous OC to unload vehicles in four minutes and to throw loads out of the vehicles pell-mell'.[10] Not for the first time George must have been thankful that he managed to become a dispatch rider.

15 August 1943

I think I'll make myself a bed, the ground seems a bit hard and stony sometimes. It all depends on how tired one is. We could do with the nice spring beds that we had near Benghazi.

22 August 1943

I have sent some lemons and a few nuts, oranges and pomegranates and I shall be interested to know what condition they arrive in. We sometimes get some grapes, pears, plums, blackberries, strawberries, oranges and figs and stew them all up together. We are doing very well for grub. Joey is our cook and is very good at it too.

Many of George's letters from Sicily mention that he was sending home parcels of nuts and lemons, and sometimes oranges and other fruits. As his letters could still take up to two months to arrive, one wonders what state the contents were in, if and when a parcel arrived. Although fruit was never rationed during the war, exotic fruit such as bananas disappeared from the shops and oranges were only occasionally seen. A parcel of oranges, therefore, would have been a rare treat for the children, but Jean has no recollection of receiving any fruit, only some almond nuts too hard to crack. His letter continued:

I had a swim in a fresh water reservoir last night – it seemed a bit colder than the sea and was quite refreshing. There is an elaborate irrigation system to supply water for the orchards and fields. The water comes down from the reservoirs, which are fed by springs, through narrow concrete channels raised from the ground by stone walls. The water is diverted from one channel to another, so they can flood whichever field or orchard they want to quite easily. We have had no rain since being here but I think that when it does rain it comes down in torrents. The orchards have stone walls around to keep the soil from running away. Soon after we fixed our tents in the orchard we were very nearly flooded out, but now we are on a bit of ground that is higher than the rest so we should be alright – that is unless they turn the water on and forget to turn it off again, in which case we will be flooded like we were in Benghazi.

27 August 1943

It is so beautiful here after so long in the dreary desert. Wouldn't I love to take you for a walk through the trees of our orchard, up as far as the reservoir where we could have a swim – '*al la nude*' of course – and then a clamber over the escarpment and then ...

Sometimes of an evening I play with the kiddies, and there are some lovely little girls that remind me so much of our Jean and Julie, and do you know what they like the best is when I swing them right up in the air like I used to with Jean and Julie. The kids are good, in fact better than the grown ups, for making us understand the lingo. Last evening I had a tinkle on a mandolin. The people here seem to have a limited understanding of music. They know the tunes from Verdi's operas such as Trovatore, Rigoletto, Traviata, Puccini's Tosca, La Bohème and Madame Butterfly, but they don't seem to know any of the German classics or any Jazz tunes, but one that seems to tickle them is 'OK Mama Get that Man for Me'.

2 September 1943

All is quiet and peaceful. The weather is warm and sunny and although some-times a few clouds pass overhead so far we have had no rain. We still get plenty to eat but very little in the way of beer ... and what little bit of chocolate we manage to get we usually pass on to the kids. Most of the kids run about on bare feet with just a little dress on and some of the bambinos are entirely with-out clothes. From a very early age they seem to have to care for themselves.

It's hardly surprising that all was quiet and peaceful in the Sicilian orchard as the German Army had left Sicily in the middle of August. On 31 August, the Italians had signed an armistice with the Allies. This, however, was not made public until 8 September. The news was greeted with wild rejoicing by the Sicilians, who had little love for Mussolini or enthusiasm for the war. One young officer in the Durham Light Infantry recalled being overwhelmed by ecstatic Sicilians, kissing him, patting him on the back, and shouting over and over again, '*Finito, tutto finito.*'[11]

9 September 1943

I expect the good news has cheered you all up. I don't feel half as far away from home as I used to.

But there was bad news too for, on the same day that the Italian armistice was announced, the Germans took over the port of Salerno on mainland Italy. The determination of Patton to reach Messina first, the lack of coordination between him, the US command and the Eighth Army, and the failures in planning had

19. The Drive for Messina, 10 July–17 August 1943. On 5 August, a civilian resident of
Misterbianco, near Catania, paints the slogan 'Viva England' on a wall after the village
had been occupied by the Eighth Army. (*Sgt Drennan, IWM NA 5450*)

allowed the Germans to retreat to the mainland relatively unscathed. The Allies
would now have to continue to fight their way through one defensive line after
another in their slow and bloody advance north.

The Eighth Army had already started on that campaign. They had crossed the
Strait of Messina on 3 September with Montgomery, who was as ever concerned
to minimise casualties among his men. He ensured that their advance was
preceded by heavy bombardment – 600 Eighth Army guns, 400 tons of ammunition, and gunfire from three battleships, destroyers and gunboats. Then, on 9
September, the US 5th Army began attacking Salerno.

These moves were not yet to uproot George, Bill and Joey, who were now living comfortably and enjoying an abundance and variety of food that could only be dreamed about by their families back home. George's letter of 9 September continued:

> We are building a house with petrol tins filled with dirt, with a tin roof, which will be better for us in case we are here when the rainy season comes. We have also made a jolly good oven with stones and a 44-gallon petrol barrel. We had a bottle of beer last night, the second since being here, but we do get hold of a drop of good wine sometimes ...

19 September 1943

We are having a nice rest in pleasant surrounding, though I shall be quite ready when the time comes for us to push on again on the next stage towards home and you. Bill, Joey and I are still together in our little house and we each have made a bed. I am writing by lamp light on our home-made table. The house is built around two almond trees so we have two tree trunks rising from the concrete floor through the roof. We have mosquito netting over the windows and the door to keep out the flies.

We are doing well for grub with Joey as our cook. Last night we had a special 'do' and invited several of our pals – those lads who were with us at Brighouse. We had soup, roast beef, roast potatoes, carrots, onions, Yorkshire pudding, followed by a steamed pudding with custard, and then rice pudding and peaches. We then had plain cake, fruitcake, custard tart, oatmeal toffee, almonds and raisins for tea, followed by wine and a singsong.

I bought a mandolin for £1 and may get a fiddle sometime but haven't seen one yet. Another bloke has a guitar which I use mostly as he cannot play it. We managed to smuggle the music and the gramophone over, which was good going as we travelled very light.

Of course, life for George, Bill and Joey may not have been quite as easy as these letters make out. Yet again he says nothing about the difficulties or dangers of his working days: nothing about riding over rough roads in the heat and dust with land mines left by the retreating army. Other less fortunate soldiers met with nasty devices such as castrators, which if trodden upon would shoot up the leg and through the body, or Bouncing Betties, which when detonated could kill anyone within 30 yards.[12]

Later in November George did admit that he hadn't had a day's leave for about a year – so he must have been working hard. But the work of the labourers at the petrol depot would have been harder. In Egypt 'native labour' was engaged to do the heavy work of unloading, decanting and loading fuel; in Targia Basotho soldiers of the Royal African Pioneer Corps performed these menial tasks and were paid less than men of similar rank for doing so. We tend to think of the Eighth Army as essentially British, but it was in fact a multinational fighting force, with contingents from the Dominions and other allies. Rates of pay and conditions of service, however, were not the same. The African soldiers were paid least, and those serving with the South African forces not only were paid less than their fellow combatants, but also faced a colour bar in their NAAFI

III. The Royal African Pioneer Corps Does the Dirty Work

In 1941 soldiers were recruited from the High Commission territories – today Botswana, Lesotho and Swaziland – to serve in the Royal African Pioneer Corps. They were, in theory, volunteers. Described and treated as tribal levies, they were recruited originally to do the hard pick-and-shovel work of a pioneer corps, though later in the war some of them moved into offensive warfare including artillery. But 'tribal levy' gives a misleading picture: many had worked in the mines of South Africa, were used to living a tough and disciplined life in barracks, and had nothing to learn about picks and shovels.[13]

In Sicily Basotho soldiers were doing the heavy work in the petrol depot. Later, in Naples, they were brought in to do the heavy work on the guns. Richard Hoggart, whose ack-ack regiment was then guarding the battered harbour at Naples, recalled, 'They had a minor chief with them, a courteous man who paid proper attention to their cultural rights, beginning with their precise preparation of their food, which was chiefly in the form of ground meal. They slept in separate tents. The English gunners said their body sweat made them smell like horses; their leader told us mildly that the English smelt like mouse droppings.'[14]

It was a long war for the pioneers; many did not return home until 1946. Daily rates of pay were low (as were those for other African soldiers): 1s 6d, with 9d of it deferred, for a single private, and 2s 3d for a private with dependants, of which 9d was paid, 9d went to the dependant, and 9d was deferred. The deferred pay was increased by 1d a day in 1945.[15] Some, at least, were treated less than generously. Three decades later Thousand Bome, who had served in the corps and was then a driver for Botswana Extension College, told Jean's husband, with lingering resentment, how on demobilisation soldiers from South Africa were each given a plough, because they were treated as volunteers, while those from Botswana did not, because they had been sent by their chief.

canteens.[16] Men from the Royal African Pioneer Corps were at the bottom of the hierarchy and, at this stage in the war, were not deployed on combat duties but were relegated to labouring jobs (see box opposite). The following account describes the work of pioneers from Bechuanaland (now Botswana) at another unnamed petrol depot:

> Some sections ... were employed at a petrol depot, unloading, decanting, filling and loading petrol. Ninety men, when the work at the depot was piling up, washed cans for 78,000 gallons, filled them and then stacked them or loaded them on to transport for the front in one day; later 120 men accounted for 50,000 gallons in five hours, and seventy men accounted for 57,000 gallons in 4-gallon cans in one day.[17]

It was tough work and thirsty work, but they were tough men, many of whom had worked in the mines of South Africa. The war diary records that, on 22 September, some of the Basotho labourers at the Targia depot caused a disturbance by 'beating up' farmers who would not sell them wine.[18]

23 September 1943
> During the last two or three days I have had 14 airmail post cards and 2 airgraphs ... We have had a letter from Cliff and after having had a rather too exciting time on the ambulance job he has been taken off for a rest. He would very much like to get back with us.

George often listed the dates of the postcards and letters, so that Maud would know which he had received and which had gone astray. This batch of mail from home had taken over two months to arrive. His next letters home are brief, no more than hurried notes, for he had to leave his little house in the orchard to take part in a mission to Catania to find a new site for the depot. The war diary tells us that the detachment, which set out on 26 September, included two officers, twenty-four other ranks, two 3-ton lorries and one motorcycle – George's Matchless 943123. Bill was not included in this party.[19] After being immobilised by thunderstorms in early October, they moved between the railheads of Catania and 'Bicoccia' (presumably Bicocca, a few miles south of Catania) trying to find a suitable site, and ended up at Catania:

6 October 1943
> I am not with Bill and Joey now having left them a little bit behind but I see them about once a week. Things are not quite so easy. I have some fairly long journeys over rough roads but I'm doing alright. We had been sleeping in bivvies until the rains came. Now we are in farmhouse buildings. I have a little

room to myself which I have cleaned up, fixed the window, put a 'mossie' net over the door, fixed up an electric light from a generator nearby, laid down a couple of planks for my bed, cemented over a little hole in the far end. There is just room for me to lie out straight with my kit at one end. Have you guessed? It is the 'gib' house.[20]

It seems he had made himself comfortable in an Arabic lavatory. The mossie net was a sensible precaution, since malaria was rife in the low-lying plain of Catania and it is estimated that malaria claimed more victims among the troops than did the fighting.[21]

24 October 1943

I haven't written much lately. I don't seem to have been able to manage it, but I have been thinking of you all the more. I always do when I don't get a chance to write ... I sometimes wonder whether it has been worth it ... I see all around poverty and disease ... I cannot say that I have a great deal of pity for the grown-up people. I feel that they had something to do with me being away for so long, but what does hurt me is the condition that some of the little children are in – little babies covered in sores and obviously either underfed or not getting the right food. When I see these things, then I realise it has been worth it for I feel that I have done my share in helping to keep such conditions from our little girls and from you. I would rather spend the rest of my life here than anything like that should happen to you.

14 November 1943

After having had a fairly busy time the past two months I am finding things much easier. I get more time off and have been to the pictures several times. You mention that you have sent soap and money. I have about 10 bars of 'Lux' soap in my bag and can get plenty more when I want it. I am also about £20 in credit so I don't need money.

We have been having a lot of rain. Sometimes in the wet weather I have been a wee bit fed up with the job but I don't know any other job here that I would prefer to do. It gets me about and I can do very much what I like. Most of the blokes around seem to have monotonous jobs, which wouldn't suit me.

21 November 1943

Well what do you think Darling? It is Sunday and I have got the day off, the first since my leave last year. I shall go to a forces place which has recently been opened, where there is a nice little band comprising violin, piano, bass drums, saxophone, trumpet and vocalist, and where we can get tea and ice cream. Then after lunch I am going to a symphony concert. This orchestra is here today only, so that it is a stroke of luck for me. One piece I know that is being played is Schubert's 'Unfinished'. Then tonight I shall be with the lads and shall probably go to the pictures.

A later letter gave details of the programme, a cornucopia of popular pieces, including Beethoven's *Coriolanus Overture*, the intermezzo from Mascagni's *Cavalleria Rusticana*, Mozart's *Turkish March*, the overture to Rossini's *The Italian Girl in Algiers*, the first movement of Schubert's 'Unfinished Symphony' the first and second movements of Beethoven's Fifth, the prelude to act one of Verdi's *La Traviata*, a Boccherini minuet, and, finally, Verdi's *Sicilian Vespers*. We do not know which orchestra it was, but George mentioned that there were thirty-five players and they played well. While in Sicily the troops were also entertained by well-known entertainers, the pop stars of their day, including George Formby and Gracie Fields, but it was the less well-known ones who had braved the more primitive conditions of the desert that earned George's gratitude.

The same letter of 21 November described how, a little while before, he had taken an unscheduled detour on his bike up to the snowline on Mount Etna, the massive volcano that lies to the north of Catania that has been more or less active for at least 2,500 years:

I had to go to a place 7,000 feet up a mountain but I was told that the last part I wouldn't be able to do on a motorbike, so I would probably have to climb it on foot. However, I am all for getting on a bit of fresh ground and if I was told to go to Timbuktu I'd have a go at getting there. So I started off climbing steadily, and then when I left the last little village I was more often in second gear than any other. Then I was passing masses of lava and getting some marvellous views when swinging round the bends and there didn't seem to be a soul about – that's the time when I'm nearest to you and I can almost imagine you are on the back. More than once I found myself talking to you. Well by this time it was pretty chilly but fortunately I was well prepared for the cold ... On several occasions I had to pull up where the road has been blown up and one time just before I got to my destination I arrived at a place where a bridge was down and I had to turn back several miles before I found a diversion, and my goodness what a diversion it was. It went nearly straight up, and there were loose rocks all the way up, but eventually I got to the top feeling as if I'd just had a couple of rounds with Joe Louis.

When I had finished at my destination I found that it was possible to get up further still so I couldn't resist the temptation and up I went about another 2,000 feet where I was among the snow. I would have liked to get to the summit but it was impossible to go any further on the bike and time was getting on. And I knew that if I had a slip and sprained an ankle or something I would never last the night. There was no one about and I thought well I've got three little girls waiting for me, and so I came back and the old bike ran perfectly both ways.

Where and why was George sent on this mission? Baedeker, writing a decade before, noted that apart from the village of Maletto at about 3,000 feet, there were only a few isolated farmhouses above 2,900 feet and none beyond 4,565 feet. He describes the way up from Nicolosi to the Casa Cantoniera, a refuge built by the Italian Alpine Club to facilitate winter ascents of the mountain, but warns against attempting Etna in winter when alpine equipment is needed and the guides are unwilling to go.[22] George sent home a postcard showing the Casa Cantoniera on the southern flank of Etna at 6,177 feet, with the bleak inhospitable slopes rising up to the volcanic cone of the Montagnola. Perhaps he stopped first at the Cantoniera and then ventured further up the track towards the observatory, which at that time stood just below the central crater?[23] But was the Cantoniera an official destination? Maybe this trip did not have a military purpose – after all, the fighting in Sicily was over? One of George's stories, in later years, was of an occasion when, having taken a message to a ladyfriend of the commanding officer, he went on to explore a volcano, confident that he could get away with such a detour. Jean had always assumed that this story related to a trip up Vesuvius, but maybe it was on Mount Etna – although this would seem a curious place for an amorous assignation.

Sull'Etna - La Cantoniera con la Montagnola (m. 2644) sullo sfondo.

20. Casa Cantoniera on the slopes of Etna.

While the detachment was exploring the area near Catania with a view to establishing a petrol depot there, the Allies were continuing to push northwards through Italy. The Eighth Army was making its way from Messina up the Adriatic coast of Italy, while on 5 October the US 5th Army, after landing at Salerno, had taken Naples. Montgomery records that the initial landing by the Eighth Army went well, but by end of October very heavy rain set in so that the vehicles could scarcely move in the chocolate sauce. Petrol became scarce and many vehicles were in need of repair. Sicily too was experiencing torrential rain that winter:

9 December 1943

I've never seen it rain so hard in my life and wouldn't have thought it possible. The hills are like cataracts of water tearing down and sometimes I have to plough my way across a street expecting to be washed away any minute. I have seen the rush of water going over the tops of cars. When it's like that of course, it isn't long before my bike is full of water. Well darling although I have got a bit damp on occasions I haven't had any colds ... [and] before you get this I shall be back with Bill and Joey.

Despite the apparent geographical advantages of Catania, with its port, airfields and a rail links – north to Messina, south to Syracuse and beyond, and inland to the north and south coasts – and a potential site for a depot within 500 yards of the docks, it was decided that setting up here would not be viable.[24] And so the detachment returned to Targia on 17 December, according to the war diary, but George's letters imply he may have got back a few days later.[25]

18 December 1943

The weather is a bit damp again but I shan't be getting wet like I used to as I have got some new kit that should keep it out ... I have bought a banjo as my old mandolin fell to pieces through the damp weather.

21 December 1943

I told you that I should be back again with Bill and Joey before Christmas and so I am and I find that they had a bed made for me and everything ready for me to move in right away.

I have tried to find something to send the kids for Christmas and for Jean's birthday but it seems hopeless ... [so] I have sent off a P.O. for our Jean and one for our Julie so that she wouldn't feel hurt at not having anything.

The war diary entry for Christmas Day that year was typically brief: 'Owing to shipping loading programme being completed work closes in depot for

Christmas Day. Officers serve men Xmas Dinner of Pork and Turkey'.[26] It appears that, in fact, the officers shirked their traditional duty that year and left it to two sergeants. But the men had no reason to complain about the fare:

26 December 1943

[On Christmas Day] I was really on duty and had to go out several times and the roads were a bit tricky as there is plenty of mud about ... Our Christmas dinner was a great success and we were waited on by two sergeants. We started off with cocktails and beer, followed by grapefruit, soup, fish, then some concoction with eggs and peas, then turkey or chicken with Yorkshire pudding, spuds, peas, beans, roast pork, apple sauce, stuffing, and then Christmas pudding and custard followed by trifle, mince pies, sausage rolls, biscuits etc.

The menu, which Bill sent home to his wife, described this feast somewhat more formally – the concoction with eggs and peas being '*a puree la peas et oeuf et mint*'. George's letter continued:

Afterwards my banjo was on the go most of the time and sometimes the guitar. We had beer, wine, marsala with eggs, and ordinary marsala, vermouth, and a small drop of whisky. I stuck to beer. I've got quite a decent banjo and gave £3.10.0 for it. It is just the job for getting the lads singing and is quite easy to play and doesn't take up much room.

£3 10s was a large sum but well spent, as banjos, ukuleles and banjoleles were the popular instruments to accompany such singsongs. George Formby, who used to accompany himself on the banjolele or the Hawaiian ukulele while singing 'When I'm Cleaning Windows' and other mildly risqué songs, was said to be a more important morale booster than Churchill.[27] The Christmas singing included another stirring song, 'Lili Marlene', which was to be the unofficial anthem of the Eighth Army:

30 December 1943

When I sent you the words and tune of the song Lily Marlene, I wrote it down in the wrong key and the words also were a very rough translation – at the time I had only heard it once and had never seen the music or a proper translation. [It's] very popular out here.

31 December 1943

Since I have been back with Bill and Joey life has seemed easy and I've got time to play my banjo. We have got plenty of music so don't send me any more, especially as I can quite easily play tunes with it from memory. I can also take off some strings and tune it up like a ukulele.

The usual 'American banjo' had five strings, but George's new banjo must have had more – maybe six, seven or even nine strings. One string, the chanterelle or melody string, would be tuned to a much higher pitch than the others and played with the thumb, while the lower strings were strummed to provide a simple accompaniment. The ukulele, essentially a small guitar, has four strings (as does the banjolele). George had to leave his ukulele behind in Egypt, but when he needed one he could make do by removing the surplus strings from the banjo and tuning it up to a higher pitch.

After that splendid Christmas there is a gap in the letters during the first half of the new year. Perhaps George was busy again in preparation for the impending move north. More probably his letters never arrived for it looks as if that January was actually an easy time with training courses and educational sessions laid on to keep the men occupied. The war diary reveals that George was among those required to attend a three-day course that month. The programme for 8 January started at 8.30 a.m. with PT and foot drill, followed by weapons training, rifle drill, and anti-gas training, and then after lunch came lectures on anti-gas, military law, censorship regulations, postal regulations, military welfare services, pay, allowances and allotments. One wonders how many men managed to stay awake through all that. The unit must also have been short of paper as well as short of things to do, for during January the war diary was written on paper headed, '*Partito Nazionale Fascista, Federazione dei fasci di combattimento di ... Cartella Personale del ...*'[28]

There was time, too, for educational lectures and discussions, based on the pamphlets produced by the Army Bureau of Current Affairs. The bureau's pamphlets were designed to introduce the troops to a wide range of social and political subjects, not just the mere practicalities of settling back into a home and a job (see box on page 139). They were delivered regularly, and army regulations required that a discussion session, based on them and led by an appointed officer, should take place once a week. But this is the first time George mentioned such sessions, and it would appear that they took place only when there was nothing much else for the men to do.

14 January 1944

Sometimes when things are a bit easy we get together and have an ABCA discussion (Army Bureau of Current Affairs) and the last thing we talked about was 'What would be average man's attitude or reactions on his return to civvy life?' Will he be content to return and settle down to the old humdrum life again as though he had never left it? Of course we would all of us just jump at the chance of shoving on a suit of plus fours but at the same time I think it quite possible that a lot of men will have the wanderlust come back to them, especially after a quiet and peaceful spell at home. As for me, I always welcome a change, but the next time I go travelling I want my missus and her two young-uns along with me.

If only things were normal I know we could be happy right here under the sunny sky, by the blue sea (it is rough just now) and the pretty scenery where the lemons and oranges are there just for the picking. I am living quite a country sort of life right now – early to bed and early to rise and a nice cold wash under a tap at the crack of dawn. We are all very particular about keeping ourselves clean. If you have lice you stand a good chance of getting typhus – rats carry it and we often have them scuttling about and running over our beds.

George must have known that his days in Sicily among the oranges and lemons were coming to and end, and that they would soon be on the move. So, yet again, he pleads with Maud not to send any more parcels.

16 January 1944

I've just had a first aid outfit from Mum, which arrived safely. I've got so much ointment, bandages and stuff now that I'm thinking of opening a chemist's shop. It all started from me asking for one tin of Germolene. I've a good mind to ask you for a bottle of beer, then I bet you would send me a brewery.

22 January 1944

I've arranged to have £20 sent home from my credits but as it's being done through the army I expect it will take a long time.

28 January 1944

I've got everything I need so please don't send me *anything*, because I haven't got room ... [and] don't worry it you don't hear from me much. I'll be getting nearer to you all the time.

At the beginning of January Montgomery had been called away to command the 21 Army Group, the British forces which, with the Americans, would open up the second front in Normandy. The main body of the Eighth Army, under its new commander General Leese, was by now well north of Naples, but was held up at Cassino where the Germans were entrenched around the town, blocking the main highway to Rome. The Allies began their attack on Cassino on 17 January. It was the first of four bloody battles that would be fought over the next four months to gain control of the town and its fortress-like Benedictine monastery, which, mistakenly it seems, was thought to be heavily guarded by

German troops. In the hope of breaking the deadlock, British and American forces had landed at Anzio on 22 January, behind the German lines and only about 30 miles south of Rome. That move didn't help. Churchill is reported as commenting, 'I had hoped that we were hurling a wild cat on the shore, but all we got was a stranded whale.'[29] The American commander, hesitant to push forward, gave the Germans time to mount a counter-attack, and his forces had to be rescued by troops from the main front.[30] It would be nearly four months before the Allies made it to Rome.

Meanwhile, however, after heavy bombing, the Allies had secured Naples, giving them access to one of the best harbours in the Mediterranean and good rail links to other parts of Italy: an ideal location for importing and distributing fuel. And so, with the action now taking place well north of Naples, it was time for the petrol depot to move. On 29 January the unit was instructed to make its way to Salerno, just south of Naples. The relatively comfortable stay that George, Bill and Joey had enjoyed in their orchard home came to an end in the early hours of 2 February 1944.

6

The San Carlo Opera Company Is Still Singing

The journey north was cold and wet. The war diary tells us that the men of the petrol depot left Targia on the morning of 2 February and drove to a transit camp in Messina where they found 'good facilities and a hot meal'. On the way one driver was involved in an accident; no one was injured but the front wheel and forks of a motorcycle were damaged. The following day they crossed the Straits of Messina by ferry to Reggio and on to a staging area at 'Sanbiase' where they 'found excellent accommodation in a thermal spa establishment'.[1] The convoy moved on again the next day, up the western side of Italy to the coastal town of Praia a Mare, and continued over difficult roads in atrocious weather via Salerno to their destination, Casoria, a small town just outside Naples. There, on 6 February, the convoy took over an existing petrol depot on the town's racecourse, with plenty of space for stocks of fuel and containers and situated next to the railway line that led down to the docks. The following day George sent Maud the usual telegram to say that he was 'safe and well' and his letters soon began again.

10 February 1944

It is raining, hailing and sleeting most of the time and there's lots of mud to contend with. We were living in a Bell tent but as it leaked like a sieve we managed to get it changed for a better and bigger one. I've been in the army over three years now and I can stand a bit of discomfort better now than before. If I want to make myself very happy I can think of my grand little wife and her two lovely young-uns.

The officers, of course, could not be expected to put up with leaky tents and plans were already afoot to ensure that they would be accommodated in more comfort. The mayor of the adjacent town, Afragola, was asked to requisition a large block of flats, half a mile away from the company headquarters, and to prepare them for occupation. George's letter continued:

We are doing well for food ... I did get together a parcel of chocolate to send home for our young ones, but now we must not send home any of the goods that have been sent out from England, for they say we need them. I have smuggled an odd bar or so in with some fruit, which I hope you get. I don't eat the stuff – I can't when I see the children here who really need it, and not only chocolate but above all bread.

16 February 1944

We are now allowed to say that we are in Italy. We travelled up by road all the way. Bill, Joey and I were the busiest of the lot but we did the job OK except for a slight mishap on Joey's part. One of the most uncomfortable parts of the journey was when we got soaked in the pouring rain and then the road went on winding up and up into the mountains until we were in the snow and our clothes were just about frozen on us. I think the one thing that kept us going was an occasional nip out of a bottle of Johnny Haig which our good hearted SQMS had handy whenever it was possible for us to partake. Driving was a bit tricky, especially at the rear where the speed is either too slow or too fast. The whisky at one point made me very happy and a little bit dizzy but by now I ride a motorbike more by instinct and what little skids I had didn't fetch me off.

The kind quartermaster was, of course, breaking army rules in giving the men swigs of whisky, for only officers were allowed to drink spirits. George's letter went on to describe another consolation when they stopped for the night at a spa – almost certainly the spa of Carontes at Sambiase (not Sanbiase as recorded in the war diary) in the Calabrian commune of Lamezia Terme:

The scenery at times was magnificent and had it been summer instead of winter I would dearly have loved you to have been with me – but it's no fun riding in a blizzard. One night we had a lovely surprise ... most of us were chilled right through and we pulled up at night at a building where we actually slept on wooden bunks. But the great part about it was that we all had a lovely warm sulphur bath. We each went down into a cellar, pulled out a plug in the wall and out came the lovely warm water which seemed to put fresh life into us.

17 February 1944

Today we moved into a building so now we can get our blankets and clothing really dry.

I am in the best of health but ever so busy, so please don't get anxious if you don't hear from me so much.

1 March 1944

There isn't much mail coming through these days – not for anyone – hope it gets better soon.

During the second half of February George's letters were unusually brief and uninformative. We don't know what journeys were keeping him so busy, but we do know that the heavy rain, which must have made his driving hazardous

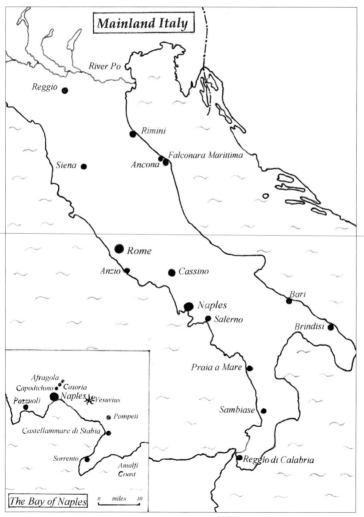

D. Mainland Italy.

and unpleasant, was also hindering work at the depot. On 11 February, the war diary notes, the rain had made three-quarters of the site unworkable and, again on 26 February, it records: 'Heavy rains during night and morning turn Depot into quagmire. Main road through Depot is only road useable. Civilian labour refused to work in wet weather.'[2]

Whereas in Sicily the hard work of the depot was done by Basotho soldiers, in Casoria it fell to local men and women. At the beginning of March, 309 men were employed as labourers. Later that month women were also taken on and by the end of the month the civilian work force had grown to 600, mostly labourers, half of whom were women. The officer in command of the depot at this time, Major Needham, appears to have been a stickler for detail. An operational instruction, issued the following month, specified precisely how the MT 80 (containers) should be re-stencilled: 'Figure 80 in red paint will be stencilled in 2" exactly in centre of 4" background. *This task is most important and will be carried out expeditiously and correctly.*'[3] Seven weeks later, after 250,000 4-gallon tanks had been re-stencilled, they ran out of paint and this 'important' work stopped.

George and Bill's journeys, presumably, took them away from such tedious jobs. When they were back at base they could start to make themselves more comfortable.

5 March 1944

Bill and I and two other drivers have been busy during easy moments building a little hut near the office where we can shelter, and now it is finished we can reap the reward. We have built in a fireplace and we can get plenty of wood and scrounge a bit of coal. Now we can dry our clothes a bit better. The fire often smokes us out when the wind blows the wrong way but we'll soon fix that.

20 March 1944

I am at a rest camp for 72 hours – the first bit of leave since just before Alamein. I am the first one to get it and the only one from our lads. It's a funny thing but as soon as I got here I felt tired so I went to bed early last night but couldn't sleep a wink. You see it was a spring bed with a mattress – in fact I nearly got out of bed and rolled myself in a blanket on the floor.

George's break appears to have given him time to reflect, somewhat ruefully, on how his wife was proving to be smarter at some things than he was. In a previous letter he had commented:

I am pleased to hear that they asked you to become an insurance canvasser, but I am glad you didn't take it because I don't want you to do too much and I'd like you to spend as much time as possible with the kids.

Napoli - La nuova stazione marittima.

21. Postcard from Naples: the New Maritime Station before it was bombed.

Napoli - Mergellina.

22. Naples: the Mergellina harbour in more peaceful days .

But it seems that she did take on more work, for his 20 March letter went on to say:

> You know you are beating your old man at his own game – poor old me was
> only an agent and now my little wife is an official. Goodness knows what my
> position in the home is going to be. It strikes me I might be bustling round the
> house frying the eggs and bacon, getting the kids off to school and the old girl
> off to business or perhaps I might be engaged as your chauffeur when you get
> a car. Oh well – don't work too hard and don't take things too seriously.

That would, indeed, have been a more efficient division of labour between them
in post-war years. George was a far better cook than Maud, for he cared about
his food. Meals for Maud were essentially refuelling stops, to be dealt with as
simply and quickly as possible before moving on to more important things – a
walk on the downs or a swim in the sea. She also had a better head for accounts
and was more outgoing and confident in dealing with people and, hence, more
successful at persuading them to take out insurance policies.

> *22 March 1944*
>
> Just got back from my 72-hour leave ... I stayed at a nice place in the middle of
> a large town and everything was very comfortable ... I went to the opera house
> one afternoon and heard *Madame Butterfly*, which was good.

Naples, the large town that he was so careful not to name, had been more
severely devastated by the Allied bombing than any other Italian city – its port
facilities and rail links had been prime targets. The monumental new Maritime
Station had been destroyed and 130 ships lay wrecked in the harbour. The city's
sewage and water systems had been blown up by the departing Germans, who
had also left booby traps and delayed action mines. Many of its citizens were living in poverty, and typhus was rampant in the streets.[4] But the Teatro San Carlo,
bombed the previous year, had already been restored and the San Carlo Opera
Company was still singing.

> *[?] March 1944*
>
> I've had and forgotten my 72-hour break. It was alright for the start but I guess
> that I had too much time to think and I began to get a bit lonely and found that
> I was pining for my wife and kids. So I was happier when I got back to work,
> although the roads were wet and greasy. Now I feel happy as a sand boy, and
> the weather has cleared up making the job seem easy. It certainly does seem as
> though spring is in the air, for the sunshine is glorious, but it is changeable for
> yesterday it tried to snow a bit ... I've seen a wonderful sight just recently but
> can't tell you about it till I get home.

In March that year the inhabitants of the Naples area witnessed a prolonged and spectacular firework display. Mount Vesuvius, which had destroyed Pompeii in AD 79, maintains a pattern of violent eruptions between long periods of relative quiescence. It had been fairly well-behaved since 1906, but in March 1944 it exploded violently again and continued spewing out mushroom clouds of smoke and ash for seventeen days. The rivers of molten lava lit up the streets at night and helped the Germans in their nightly bombing raids on the port. Norman Lewis wrote:

> It was the most majestic and terrible sight I have ever seen, or ever expect to see. The smoke from the crater slowly built up into a great bulging shape having all the appearance of solidity. It swelled and expanded so slowly that there was no sign of movement in the cloud which, by evening, must have risen thirty or forty thousand feet into the sky, and measured many miles across.[5]

George, with his meticulous respect for the censor's rules, presumably felt that any reference to the eruption would have revealed his whereabouts, and so he must talk of less exciting things:

3 April 1944

Many thanks for the cycling snaps – I think they are grand – and three nice blue handkerchiefs which will come in handy. I left nearly all my hankies

23. Jean and Julie on their bikes.

behind in Egypt. I should have thought that by now our personal things would have been sent on but I expect I shall have to wait until the war is over.

7 April 1944

I've got a little girl named Lida who pops in to see me sometimes in our little shack. She is four years old and such a tiny thing that one wouldn't imagine her to be more than two. The way she looks at me with her pretty little face makes me feel she is short of a little bit of love – as I am – and we are great pals.

In an undated letter to Jean and Julie, he also wrote about Lida who he was able to befriend and comfort in the way that, in today's sex-obsessed society, men feel they dare not for fear of being accused of paedophilia:

Daddy has a little Italian girl friend. Her name is Lida and she is four years old. Unfortunately she hasn't been getting enough to eat and she can't be any bigger than our Julie was when she was two years old, and her little arms and legs are very thin. She loves to sit beside your Dad on a seat in his hut and she

24. A little Italian girl holding an umbrella watches a despatch rider attempt to clear the carburettor of his motorcycle in torrential rain, 4 October 1943. (*Lt Chetwyn, IWM NA 7526*)

loves Dad to put his arm around her. I don't suppose she has anyone to give her much love. I am going to try to feed her up so that she is a bonny lass like my Jean and Julie. We are getting on ever so well with talking to each other. Of course Dad has to speak in Italian to her.

Among George's letters were two well-thumbed phrasebooks. It seems that he was making a serious attempt to learn some Italian so that he could communicate with his little friends. His sympathy, however, did not extend to their parents.

13 April 1944

I've been trying for weeks to find something to send home but everything on sale is useless or ridiculously expensive that it seems mad to buy anything. We used to moan about the 'Gypoes' but these 'Ities' lick them hollow for swindling.

It seems that everyone thieved or fiddled, and often with great ingenuity. Norman Lewis, working in the Field Security Services in the Naples area in 1943, maintained, 'Nothing has been too large or too small – from telegraph poles to phials of penicillin – to escape from Neapolitan kleptomania.' He recalled that a week or two before, 'An orchestra playing at the San Carlo to an audience largely clothed in Allied hospital blankets, returned from a five-minute interval to find all its instruments missing.'[6] The thieves had even scaled the ramparts of Castellammare Castle, which housed the Field Security Headquarters for Italy, removed the wheels from all the vehicles, and escaped back with them over the 30-foot-high walls. Richard Hoggart, who was organising educational and cultural activities for the army in Naples, tells a similar story of an American supply depot in the south of the city which 'had been comprehensively robbed between 2 and 5 a.m. by little boys coming up from the sewer manholes within the depot and manoeuvring the goods through to other manholes outside the wall and so to a stream of waiting lorries'.[7]

Given the devastation and poverty in Naples at the time, who could blame them? According to Lewis, it was

astonishing to witness the struggles of a city so shattered, so starved, so deprived of all those things that justify a city's existence, to adapt into a collapse into conditions which must resemble life in the Dark Ages. People camp out like Bedouins in deserts of brick. There is little food, little water, no salt, no soap. A lot of Neapolitans have lost their possessions, including most of their clothing, in the bombings and I have seen some strange combinations of garments about the streets, including a man in an old dinner-jacket, knickerbockers and army boots, and several women in lacy confections that might have been made up from curtains. There are no cars but carts by the hundred, and a few antique coaches such as barouches and phaetons drawn by lean horses.[8]

The small towns to the north of Naples, such as Casoria where the petrol depot was now located, were similarly impoverished. 'Seen from the outside through the orchards that surround them, all these towns look attractive enough: tiny versions of Naples itself, clustered round their blue-domed churches … [but] on the inside they are the showcases of poverty and misery.'[9] Lewis concluded that, in these circumstances, his job of establishing effective security in the area was a hopeless one.

26 April 1944

Last night I went out with Bill and we wandered around some of the back streets. We soon had lots of kids asking us for chocolate and caramel, and as we had none we looked around and found a shop where we bought and filled our pockets with monkey nuts and wood nuts. Well then in a very few moments we had dozens of half-starved urchins around us and, as we found it difficult to hand the nuts out and share them properly, we threw them up in the air in handfuls and all the kids simply dived for them. One urchin had about six others jump on top of him and he must have got a bit hurt for he started crying. However, when I picked him up and filled his pockets with nuts he was as right as rain and didn't seem to think he had done so badly.

9 April 1944

We have got showers rigged up now so that I have a cold bath every day … We are pestered with flies – the ordinary house fly such as you have in England – but these are the most persistent little fellows imaginable, they settle on you all over and try to get into your mouth and ears and eyes, and when you knock them off they keep on coming until you kill them. We kill dozens every day with fly swats. It gives you a feeling of satisfaction and revenge.

The next tent had an unwelcome visitor the other day, a green scorpion, and I ran over a big black one. From now on I shall hang my boots up out of reach.

Another gap in the letters suggests that something bigger than swatting house-flies was keeping him busy: a flurry of messages, perhaps, connected with the latest attempt on Cassino. The long and bloody struggle for the fortress had been going on since January and, on 11 May, the final assault began.

14 May 1944

As you will have heard by now things have started and I hope the climax and finish will soon be over. Let me get back home, that's all I want, my wife and little kids. I think old Bill and I have done our share and its time for us to come and see what our missuses have been up to since we have been away.

Glad to hear that you have got a rise. Is it now 35/- for you and 12/6 each for the kids? I get 5/- a day, which is enough to keep me in vermouth. We get no beer at all now and I don't like the wine. The only drink I care for is vermouth or marsala. I don't have much of that. Certainly I never get drunk in this country – 'cos you know how it affects me – and I have a horror of catching one of the many diseases around.

Before this letter arrived home, Maud would have heard that, on 18 May, Cassino finally fell to the Allies. They were now able to push forward towards Rome, although not without having to battle against stiff rearguard action. But whatever relief he may have felt at the breakthrough at Cassino, a more personal matter was bothering George that day:

19 May 1944

Your letter of the 10th made me a bit uneasy and this is my second attempt at writing. I know things are very different at Rushden but I had hoped that you had managed to settle down alright. I know that some people are very narrow minded. I know that you like a bit of fun and like to be mischievous (and that is one of the reasons why I love you and always shall) but there are certain things which, although they may not be wrong, are not worthwhile doing. I know how you feel and wish I could do something to help ... I love and trust you with all my heart ... so stick your chin out and keep smiling and may this lousy war be over soon.

We cannot know what incident, or indiscretion, prompted this awkward and uncharacteristically oblique letter. Perhaps Maud had been to a social event or even a dance attended by American airmen from one of the nearby airbases and this had given rise to criticism from her mother-in-law or spiteful comments from a neighbour. The American servicemen were seen as having too much money to splash around – to ply the kids with chocolate and chewing gum and charm the pants off their mums. On one occasion an airman knocked on the door and asked for Maud – maybe she had met him at some social event the day before. On that occasion she sent him briskly away, but the two children teased her about her Yankee boyfriend.

In her letter to George, Maud would not have been writing about her worst problems – the children's illnesses or the stress of living with a narrow-minded and hostile mother-in-law – she kept those bigger problems firmly to herself. But the antagonism of her mother-in-law may well have lain below the surface of whatever lesser problem she did share with him. Annie Warner, Maud's mother-in-law and 'grandma' to Jean and Julie, was a tough little woman, a fighter for the interests of her immediate family – her three sons and four granddaughters – and fiercely intolerant of anyone who threatened their well-being. She hadn't welcomed Maud as a wife for her handsome youngest son. Maud thought this was because she was six years older than George, but probably Annie also felt uncomfortable living with a daughter-in-law who was better educated and who had decidedly more liberal views. Certainly she blamed Maud for letting George enlist, arguing that she could easily have dissuaded him from doing so. The other two sons stayed behind, living nearby and working in reserved occupations: Bob was in a munitions factory, and Dick had a prosperous business making tombstones. Annie felt that George, too, ought to have found a way of staying out of the army. Not that this implied any pacifism on her part – far from it. She was a pugnacious patriot for whom the only good German was a dead German.

Not only did Maud have to contend with the absence of her husband and the daily fear that he might be killed or injured, she had to share the small house with this strong-willed woman who had very different ideas about how to bring up children. Grandma loved and indulged her granddaughters, particularly the pretty and vivacious little Julie, but she had some odd views on suitable activities for them. She saw no problem in taking them to her regular spiritualist gatherings, where, in a darkened room, they would hold hands and seek to make contact with her dead father.

Whereas it would have been unseemly for Maud to go to a dance with a serviceman, it was perfectly acceptable for George and his mates to enjoy such pleasures:

29 May 1944

We had a unit dance the other evening in the local village hall and quite a number of the 'Itie Signorinas' came – some who work for us – but as a dance it was a bit of a wash-out because most of them couldn't dance. The dance that Bill and I went to before was in the town where everybody is more modern but the people in the country are behind the times. For instance if you wanted to take a nice country girl out you would have to take the whole darn family – just like in Victorian ages the girls can't be trusted and must be chaperoned.

Although George continued to omit any place names from his letters, it appears that it was acceptable to send picture postcards with place names on them. A postcard to Jean, dated 31 May 1944, shows the usual panoramic view of Naples. If she hadn't already guessed, Maud would now have known where he was and no doubt she was relieved that he was well behind the Italian front. She was probably pleased, for once, that George was still in Italy and not taking part in the more hazardous invasion of Normandy.

6 June 1944

So glad to hear the great news of the second front and it has bucked us all up and makes us feel that we are nearer home. My thoughts are with the lads and I do hope they will get going with few losses.

On 6 June the D-Day landings in Normandy began. By the end of that day 156,000 men had landed on the shores of France. Jean's future husband, Hilary, then nine years old and already following the news avidly, was living in Havant just outside Portsmouth. He recalls listening to news of the invasion on the radio at school that day, when it was claimed that the Allies were already heading for Caen. The class was told to look for Caen in their atlases; in fact it took many weeks of fierce fighting to liberate the town. Hilary had already seen the invasion fleet in Spithead when the family went on a day trip to the Isle of Wight – newly opened to visitors – in the spring of 1944. There were loudspeaker announcements on the paddle steamer warning against telling anyone what was to be seen – probably the usual comment, 'Careless talk costs lives.' With practically wall-to-wall vessels, the invasion fleet could not have been hidden, but the secret – that it was to sail south to Normandy, not south-east to Calais as the Germans had been led to believe – was successfully guarded.

Although unexpected, the D-Day landings were not achieved without loss of life and limb. On Omaha beach, 'Within minutes of landing, the sea was red with blood and the screams of dying men competed with the roar of artillery fire.'[10] But the landing and the subsequent progress, although slow, had raised the nation's spirits. By July 1944, according to A. J. P. Taylor, most English people decided that the war was as good as won and holidaymakers again enjoyed the beaches from which they had been excluded for five years. The renewed confidence helped them to surmount their last trial – the unnerving and deadly flying bombs that began falling on London.[11]

George's letter of 6 June did not mention the other significant military news. The day before, General Mark Clark, with troops from the American 5th Army and his cameramen in tow, made his triumphal entry into Rome. Clark had been determined that Rome should be *his* prize, and told General Alexander, his commander-in-chief, that if the Eighth Army tried to muscle in on the act, he would have his troops fire on them.[12] But in his dash for glory, Clark, like Patton in Sicily, ignored the need to work closely with the Eighth Army to cut off the retreating enemy forces. Instead, the enemy was allowed to retreat at its own pace, and so continue to hinder the Eighth Army in its slow push north. George's letter, however, went on to chat about more personal matters:

> I had another bike frame snap underneath me but I was OK – I expect I do too much rough riding ... I was a bit envious of you having a dip in the baths. Only a very few miles away is a lovely blue sea and I haven't been in once this year. Still I can't grumble, things aren't at all bad.

Midsummer and still no time to snatch a swim in the tantalising sea nearby – that, for George, was ample reason for a grumble. But the local women at the depot, humping barrels and decanting fuel in the heat and the dust, had more cause to complain, especially as they were poorly paid for this tough work. It would appear, from the war diary, they got less than eighteen old pence a day.[13] On 5 June several female labourers suffered heat strokes and fainted, and this prompted action to improve their conditions. Two days later dust control measures were introduced and work began on making 500 aprons out of unserviceable gas capes, 'to be used on such work as oil decanting by female labour'.[14] The following week the 'Hygiene Section' visited the depot to disinfect the labourers, who, coming from overcrowded homes with a shortage of soap and water, were susceptible to the typhus-carrying lice. For George, however, life was getting better:

> *25 June 1944*
>
> Well Darling I managed it – that is by a bit of wangling. I managed to get into town to hear Jascha Heifetz play the fiddle. I also saw a fellow I know there and he came along with me. The place was crammed but we managed to get quite a good seat. First he played a sonata for violin and piano by Mozart, then the Mendelssohn Concerto. After a short interval he went on to play short pieces by Ravel, Elgar, Paganini, Sarasate's *Gipsy Airs*, Mendelssohn's *On Wings of Song* and other pieces. He is certainly the most brilliant violinist I have every heard ... I felt happy enough as I speeded back on my old bike.

No wonder he sped happily back after listening to Heifetz, a violinist's violinist whose playing has been described as 'unique in luminous transparency of texture, tonal perfection, and formal equilibrium of phrasing'.[15] The Russian-born violinist was, by this time, an American citizen. He gave freely of his time to help with the war effort and to entertain the American troops. After one such concert in Italy he was invited to dine in the officers' club but chose instead to join the men in the main dining room, saying, 'I am here to be with the boys.'[16] That incident would have endeared him further to George.

Had George been in England, it is highly unlikely that he would have had a chance to listen to a live concert by a violinist of the calibre of Heifetz or to go to an opera, certainly not one to match the quality of the San Carlo Opera Company. Richard Hoggart commented that the San Carlo Opera was not yet famous and was suffering from chronic shortages of gear; *La Bohème*'s Mimi, for example, died on a brown blanket clearly marked 'US Forces'. But according to Hoggart, that didn't matter, for they had a vitality that made the Carl Rosa Company (the touring company that took opera to provincial centres in Britain) look wan. In Hoggart's experience these performances 'affected only a small minority but ran across all ranks', adding, as if this were surprising, 'I met a Cockney private who had become an enthusiast.'[17] Another low-ranking enthusiast, Driver George Warner, sent his programmes home to his wife where they were carefully preserved among his letters for another sixty years.

21 July 1944

I managed to see *La Bohème* at the Opera House and thoroughly enjoyed it. I shall be sending you a programme. Mimi, the soprano, had one of the most beautiful voices I have heard. It is true that she was rather fat and well developed when she should have been small and delicate, but I forgot that when I heard her glorious voice.

George was lucky to get to that performance as he had been extra busy covering for Bill, who was in hospital again.

26 July 1944

Bill came out of 'dock' yesterday and he is alright and helping a bit with the short runs. He will soon be running as normal and already I am getting more time to do things.

31 July 1944

I have just come back from my first swim this year – but first of all let me tell you that our kit bags have arrived from Egypt and I think all my kit has come along OK including the uke, plenty of hankies, extra woollies and my swimming trunks and snaps. My bathing drawers arrived just as arrangements had been made for us to go to a swimming bath about 10 miles away. The bath was quite a big affair about 50 yards long and almost as wide. I got into it just as quickly as I could and really enjoyed it, although I would rather have gone down to the sea. One of these days I think I shall steal a swim in the blue sea but so far there hasn't been much time.

Although George and Bill had managed to smuggle their Primus stove, gramophone and some records with them when they left Egypt, they had to leave

25. Still together:
George and Bill, August
1944.

behind other prize possessions, including the ukulele. But it is surprising that
George didn't find room for his bathing trunks.

19 August 1944

I had another day off yesterday and went to town with one of my mates. We
went to the opera to see *Rigoletto*, the first time I had seen that one, but it
wasn't as good as I expected. The next one I want to see is *Tosca* but I must
wait another fortnight for my day off ... Some band players are being sent to
our unit and I am told that a fiddle is being bought and they want me to play
it in the band.

There is an Itie house that we are invited to go to whenever we like. It isn't
posh – it only consists of two large rooms – all the houses are overcrowded
here. But they have a radio which we can use as we like. There is an old chap
and his wife and three daughters, one of whom is married and the other

two have boyfriends ... They never ask us for anything, which is so unusual, and seem to be genuinely pleased to have us. Of course we give the old chap fags etc. and they always give us a couple of glasses of wine and fruit such as peaches, pears or apples. However we usually go to the pictures when we get a chance as there is nothing much on the radio.

For over a year the unit had been without a radio. The war diary tells us that the unit's radio had been 'lost to enemy in initial stages of Sicily campaign'. They had sought help from the brigadier to obtain a replacement the previous December, but were still without a set in December 1944 when they again applied for a replacement and were put on the waiting list.[18] By now, however, George had found a far more enticing way to spend his spare time, a discovery he made while officially on duty. His previous letter explained:

When I was bowling along on my bike I discovered the most beautiful swimming place I have ever seen. It is a little rocky cove sheltered by cliffs with big flat rocks for non-swimmers and deep clear water for diving. Old Bill and I are going to try and get there on our next day off together.

26 August 1944

Well twice Bill and I have been able to manage it and been there for a swim and it was grand. I don't think many soldiers know about it because there were only a few civvies and children there and none of our mob ... we keep it dark. The water is so warm and clear and there are a number of smooth rocky islands just above the water and it is lovely to swim in and out and around them. We are going to try and get our next day off together so that we can go there officially and take our time. It would be a perfect paradise if I could only have my missus and kids here.

Although there was no chance of his missus and kids joining him for a swim, it was beginning to look as if George and Bill might soon be seeing them again as things were going well on the second front. On 25 August jubilant crowds celebrated the liberation of Paris. George's letter continued:

Poor old Jerry is about licked now. You can see a big difference between his prisoners of two or three years ago and those of today. Some of them today are boys who still ought to be with their mothers.

28 August 1944

See you before Christmas, I hope.

I'm well off for money – have got £30 in credit so I'll probably be sending some home – but I shall always keep a decent amount in case I get the chance of leave somewhere. I am having quite an easy time with plenty to eat, drink and plenty of sleep but I would like to have a move. We have been here too long.

We had a lovely time yesterday. I was on guard the previous night but it was easy and I was quite fresh when I came off at 6 o'clock. I had a wash and a shave and my breakfast straight away and, at about 7.30, Bill and I caught a fast truck for town and it wasn't long before we were bathing in the sea at our pretty little rocky cove. After a swim we did some rock climbing, which gave us a bit of excitement. Old Bill is quite good at it. In his civvy job he is used to climbing along girders so many hundred of feet up. It is a funny thing but at a tricky place where a slip would mean a hard reception on rocks down below he wasn't a bit bothered, but when he came to a place where a mistake would mean a plunge into deep water he didn't like it a bit. You see he can only swim a few strokes. I was just the opposite ...

Bill, who went down the mines on leaving school, had later worked as a scaffolder erecting cooling towers for the steel works in South Wales, so heights were no problem for him. However, when swimming in a reservoir as boy, he had become entangled in weeds and nearly drowned, and he had been afraid of water ever since.

I should think it would be a good idea for you to go to Eastbourne with the kids to see what state things are in ... It would make things so much easier to decide and arrange if only we knew (1) when the war will be over, (2) when I am coming home, (3) whether I shall stay home or not, and most important of all, (4) when shall I get out of the army ... So Darling your husband can't help you very much and you will have to do a lot of deciding yourself.

I am not with old Bill and the lads now and not at the above address. I am attached elsewhere but only for a short time I expect, and not far away so you can still write as usual ... I am getting some longer runs but I get better breaks and no guards.

The war diary gives no clues about what George might be doing on this assignment, but it does show that the depot was by now supplying fuel to places as far apart as Rome and Reggio. George's journeys may have been connected with

such supplies, or perhaps he was taking messages to General Alexander's headquarters in Siena or to American Army contacts in Rome. Longer runs could
have taken him over the Appenines to where General Leese had his tactical HQ
and where, on 21 September, the Eighth Army captured Rimini. But, he was soon
back in Casoria, where the band was beginning to take up most of his evenings.

22 September 1944

Things are quite easy now. I have been going out with the dance band lads to
several dances doing a bit of fiddling. They don't use any music and it was a bit
awkward for the start as I didn't know lots of their tunes but I'm getting used
to it now.

Up to now he and Bill had entertained their colleagues with music for informal
singsongs, and George was much more at home with the old-fashioned songs
than the newer swing and dance rhythms. But playing in the band brought a
welcome perk – it relieved him of guard duties. His letter continued:

Do you remember I told you I had my bike pinched some time ago? Well I
have been exonerated from all blame, so now I expect a new bike pretty soon.
There is a lot of stealing going on in these parts. After all I suppose this is the
country where most of the gangsters come from. I haven't got much patience
with these people and wouldn't trust them an inch. I think their silly religion
does a lot to make them what they are for it overshadows everything that they
do. The priests have always looked well clothed and well fed and most of them
wear really good quality shoes when many children and women go about bare-
footed – also quite a number of men. I have seen quite a lot of kids without any
clothes at all.

For the women working at the depot, clothing was still a problem, despite the
order back in June for a supply of protective aprons for them. The new commanding officer, Major Lockwood-Tatham, who took over from Major Needham
on 23 September, recorded his concern in the war diary:

The female labourers are invariably scantily clad, even in cold weather, and
are little inclined to work in conditions when their health may be adversely
affected [and] because their clothing, whilst very poor, is often their only, or at
the most, one of two sets. It is thought that if they had clothing that could be
washed (i.e. Denims etc.) and which, whilst not their own would be deemed
a working suit, they would be less allergic to tasks of a nature which would
normally cause them to dirty their clothing; e.g. rolling barrels in muddy
ground.[19]

He requested, therefore, 600 pairs of army surplus trousers for them. George, meanwhile, was buying jewellery for his women:

> *23 September 1944*
>
> I have just bought you a pair of coral dewdrop earrings with a splash of red at the top and a coral necklace to match. I have also got a red necklace each for Jean and Julie and a cameo brooch for Mum. These are for Christmas in case I don't get home in time. I will send them home separately in registered envelopes and then if any don't arrive please let me know and I will send another.

This time at least one of these presents arrived home, and now Jean's red necklace looks good on her pretty fair-haired granddaughter. George's letter, however, does not mention any present for his father. Although George often asked Maud or the children to give his love to his mother, and although from time to time he mentioned Maud's mother and father, he made no mention of his own father in any of the surviving letters. This is odd, for Frank was a lovable man who, unlike Annie, was quietly and tactfully supportive of his daughter-in-law. Nor, in later years, did George give any indication of an estrangement between himself and his father. It was Annie who was estranged from her husband; her fierce love for her family no longer extended to him. Frank kept out of her way and spent his days making and mending shoes in the little lean-to shed behind the outdoor lavatory. Here, among his lasts and knives and bags of leather bits, he would escape Annie's fierce tongue. The children loved to watch him, and not just because of the toffees he kept in an eyelet tin or the little green pears that would sometimes appear from a sack under the workbench. As well as bathing them on bath nights, he would mend their bicycles, and turn his hand to any other practical job that they asked of him, such as building a hutch for Julie's pet rabbit. The children benefited too from sensible, well-fitting shoes and sandals, made-to-measure for their growing feet. On one occasion Jean had set her heart on having something less sensible, some shiny black patent-leather shoes like those that Shirley Temple wore. Eventually, but disapprovingly, Frank made her a pair.

As a skilled cobbler he must have brought in a regular income. George, on the other hand, had no such marketable skill and, increasingly, was worrying about what he would be able to do when he did get home. His previous letter went on to talk about these worries:

> Darling you keep asking me about where shall we live and what shall we do when I am out of the army. Well I don't know that I mind much what we do so long as we live somewhere near pleasant countryside or the sea. I haven't the faintest idea whether my book will be any good when I come back ... There

may be some good jobs going abroad where the sun shines more often. If you have any bright ideas for making money let me have them. I don't know what I'll be good for unless it's a speed cop. I sometimes wonder whether I shall be much good for anything when I get back – what with my old woman beating me at my own job and everybody seems to think that insurance as it is now is finished. Perhaps I might get a job at hedge cutting or something. I don't even know whether I shall suit my missus and her young daughters – possibly the army has made me coarse.

George, for all his boyish bravado, was a much less self-assured person than Maud and she was proving to be a more successful insurance agent than he had been. Among the many other papers that she kept – it looks as if she never threw a letter away – was one from the Liverpool Victoria Friendly Society, for whom she worked while in Rushden. It conveyed their 'thanks and appreciation for the excellent returns' she had been making and for 'the splendid increase' in business that she was bringing in. George also had good reason to be concerned that the insurance industry might not survive the introduction of National Insurance, as foreshadowed in the Beveridge Report. He would have plenty of time to go on worrying about what else he might be able to do, for he wasn't going to get home for Christmas.

7

Python Rears Its Head and Wriggles

The Allied forces were still battling on in Northern Italy, but the foci of the war were now in Northern Europe and Southeast Asia. In Europe, throughout August and September 1944, the Allies advanced on a wide front through France and into Belgium. In the middle of August, other forces, mainly American, had landed in the South of France near Marseilles. More significantly, the Russian Army was maintaining its advance westwards, sweeping all before them. August and September saw Finland, Romania and Bulgaria succumb to the Russian onslaught. In the Far East, the Americans were focused upon defeating Japan in the Pacific, while the British, concerned with the security of India and having checked the advance of Japan into Assam, were now poised to invade Burma and recover Singapore.

Meanwhile in Italy, Alexander's forces, seriously weakened by the withdrawal of troops for the second front in Normandy and the landings in the South of France, were suffering heavy losses as they pushed slowly north towards the Po Valley. For the men of the petrol depot, still at Casoria, work continued as usual, but their minds were increasingly occupied with the question of when they would get home. And for George, at least, there were the added problems of where he would live and how he could support his family when he did get home.

23 September 1944

I suppose you will have read about demobilisation. What do you think of my chances of getting out now? I see that they don't make any distinction between the lads who have been abroad and those who have been home most of the time getting their regular leaves. There is a bit more money for us and more still for those going out east. Do you think it is worth it – shall I go?

Two more of our lads have got their papers for going home but they were out here before No. 8 Petrol Depot arrived ... When I do come home though I want to stay.

The Government, confident that the war in Europe would soon be over, had published a white paper earlier in September setting out, in general terms, its policy for repatriating troops during the period between the defeat of Germany and the defeat of Japan. It defined two categories of personnel eligible for repatriation: Class A, where eligibility depended upon length of service and age, and Class B, which applied to those who had the skills needed at home, particularly skills relating to 'the building of houses against the time when sailors, soldiers and airmen will be returning in large numbers to civil life'.[1] George was right in thinking that the scheme, which came to be called 'Python', made no distinction between home and overseas service in calculating eligibility. Nevertheless he was hopeful that he might qualify under Class A. His letter continued:

Now about the job – you are quite right when you say hang on to one job before you think of anything else ... [but] things are going to be changed in the insurance world. However, it doesn't really matter what one does to make a living provided it is an honest job. A lot of fellows are on building and they say that the most paying job (where there are quite a number of them) is the tea boy's job. These building lads tease me sometime about the old insurance racket and say that it is finished, and that they will give me a job as a tea boy. Well I wouldn't mind that when they reckon that a tea boy makes about £15 a week.

Now when the war is over I shouldn't be surprised if a number of opportunities arise for settlement in the colonies or dominions. The country that takes my fancy is New Zealand. I believe it is healthy and beautiful there and the lads that I have met seem ever so decent – not quarrelsome like some of the Australians when they have had a drink and not boastful like some South Africans.

George was never cut out to be an insurance agent. It may have seemed an ideal way of becoming his own boss before the war, but he was no salesman. He would readily dissuade his clients from taking out a policy they could not afford and he shied away from the dispiriting task of collecting the weekly premiums from people with little money to spare. The massive, ornate, mahogany-effect sideboard that he accepted in lieu of a bad debt encumbered the home until, some fifty years later, Maud finally threw it out to rot in the garden.

In any case, it was reasonable to assume that the 'insurance racket' would be finished in post-war Britain. The 1942 Beveridge Report – with aims that, as a socialist, George could wholeheartedly endorse – promised to do him out of a job by proposing a comprehensive social insurance system to protect people from poverty, whether caused by unemployment, sickness or old age. Beveridge even envisaged that insurance against funeral expenses would be included, and that industrial insurance would be taken away from the insurance companies and collecting societies and placed in the hands of a public commission. The report had been widely welcomed and received much publicity, although the ABCA's bulletin, written by Beveridge himself and issued the previous year, was hastily withdrawn on the instructions of Sir James Grigg, the secretary of state for war, as it anticipated what might never become policy.[2] The white paper of September 1944, while scaling down the scope of the benefits, did accept many of Beveridge's recommendations in principle. And although it did not accept the complete nationalisation of industrial insurance, it certainly looked as if George might not be able to make a living by collecting weekly premiums on the doorstep. With so many bomb-damaged buildings to be repaired, and new homes to be built, the prospects for a job on a building site looked far brighter.

2 October 1944

I am ever so busy just now. Bill has been driving a wagon and there has only been me on the bike. The weather has been lousy. I did close on 200 miles the other day on one trip and it rained so heavily that I was wet through before I had finished the first 10 miles. At one time the old bike simply filled up with water in the carburettor and points, but I soon got it moving again.

The weather has changed very suddenly. None of the houses out here have fireplaces ... but I expect we shall make some stoves out of oil drums again, that is if we are here much longer.

12 October 1944

Have just had the offer of five days' rest but I'm not taking it because I should either be on my own or with someone I don't know and we should be in tents without lights in a place of no particular interest ... They wouldn't let Bill come with me so I shan't bother.

Had George and Bill been allowed to go together, they would certainly have managed to have some fun, but without Bill, George preferred to be busy, even if it did mean long trips in the rain, rather than have time to worry about his future. Now that the winter was approaching, Major Lockwood-Tatham, who had taken over command of the depot the previous month, was concerned about the lack of social facilities at the depot and its effect upon morale. A note in the war diary explained that the depot was 5 miles from the amenities of Naples and had no canteen nearby; the only other amenities were an occasional mobile cinema show and the American cinema at 'Cappodighino'.[3] (This was presumably Capodichino, an American Air Force base about a mile and a half from Casoria and now the international airport for Naples.) The major therefore applied for a canteen to boost morale, but the men had already set about providing their own morale-booster:

16 October 1944

> We have done up an old ruined building and turned it into a dance hall. We had a dance there the other week but towards the end it turned out a bit rough. But the 'do' we had last night was a bit better. There were no women there and everybody really enjoyed themselves and were the best of pals throughout.

George doesn't say where they found the women whose presence, it seems, caused a rumpus at the previous dance. Up to now, it seems, the only women working at the depot were the labourers, and they could not dance, but on 15 October the unit had been offered the services of some ATS women who, the diary indicates, could be taken on as two batwomen, two mess orderlies, one officers' mess cook and one telephone board operator.[4] George's letter continued:

> We had a new recruit to our little band who plays the trumpet and plays very well indeed. We were in the dark for the start because somebody forgot the generator but when that arrived and the wine began to work things went fine. Several of the lads did some clever turns though some of the songs were (even to me) startling in their vulgarity. Old Bill and I sang a duet with the ukulele banjo, but most of the time I was fiddling. Of course on some of the hot numbers I am quite a novice and I can't say that I am very keen on them, but we play quite a lot of the good old tunes that have stood the test of time. We don't make any money out of it. If we play for officers and get paid, the money goes into the PRI for the lads.[5] But we get as much wine as we want and plenty of nice cakes, sausage rolls etc., and it's something to do. It makes some of the dreary nights slip by quickly.
>
>   Darling I haven't seen you for three years and according to the book of rules I've only got another one and a half to do. When I do get back wild horses won't tear us apart.

31 October 1944

> We have made ourselves more comfortable for the colder weather. We have made a partition in our hut so that it is smaller and cosier and we have fitted a stove so that we have a place to keep warm in and to dry our things ...

I have just swapped my bike, which was a Matchless, for a Triumph, and the latter bike seems to be very good on the wet greasy roads. I think we are going to have some new Nortons. I used to have a Norton at Benghazi and it was a reliable old bus with plenty of guts therein.

Don't work too hard. One of these days I'll meet you coming down the garden to carry that sack of spuds for you.

As well as looking after the children, making all their clothes, and working as an insurance agent, Maud had taken on an overgrown allotment soon after moving to Rushden which she shared with her brother-in-law Bob. She was not shy of hard work, but she resented bitterly the way Bob had allowed her to dig and clear the plot, reserving his energies for harvesting time.

14 November 1944

I've got the day off and I'm writing this in the Palace. This morning when I got here I first had some tea and cakes in Church Army canteen and read the paper. Then I wandered into a music shop and heard one or two good records on the radiogram and got here in time for lunch which was dehydrated spuds, greens and a rissole, and figs and custard.

The Royal Palace, which had been taken over as a club for the forces, was lavishly equipped with social facilities, but presumably the famous Neapolitan pizza was not on the menu in the canteen. There is no indication that George ever sampled local dishes, either in North Africa or in Italy. It seems the army provided solid English food, and that may well have been what the ordinary soldier expected and preferred, for it was before the days of Indian restaurants in every town and pizza parlours delivering to our doors. Food was important to George, but as a relief from bully and biscuits, it was bacon, egg and chips that he looked forward to, and not, as he would put it, 'foreign muck'. He relished simple food and enough of it, and it grieved him to see the Italian children going about scantily dressed and hungry. In a letter addressed to Jean and Julie, written on his tenth wedding anniversary, George tells of another child that he befriended:

21 November 1944

There is a little boy – he is blind in one eye, and he only has a few rags on for clothing, and no shoes or stockings. He brings Daddy a newspaper to his hut each morning, so Dad saves a bit of his breakfast for him and he goes away looking ever so pleased and grateful. Lots of little boys and girls don't go to school and haven't been for more than a year.

By now George and Bill had been abroad, without any home leave, for over three years. They anxiously watched and weighed up the chances of leave. The LIAP scheme (Leave in Addition to Python) had already been introduced, whereby those who had served overseas for three years were entitled to short-term home leave before returning to complete their service. Much as he longed to see his family, George was not keen on this if it were to be followed by a posting to Burma. His concern appears to have been well-founded. Churchill was anxious to mount an amphibious assault on Rangoon from across the Bay of Bengal, which would require men and equipment to be withdrawn from Italy or France for deployment in Southeast Asia.[6]

23 November 1944

What do you think about this home leave that is being started? I think there is a catch in it myself and I think that a big proportion of the men who get it will go out to Burma. Old Bevin stated that, as far as humanly possible, all men going out there will get home-leave first. It is about time they lowered the length of overseas service that we have to do. If we have completed our spell they don't send us to Burma, but if we come home before it is completed they could do so. Possibly they might send us as occupational troops in Germany but I think it would be possible to have your family there for that. I should think that there are thousands of blokes still in England that could be sent out to release some of the lads here. It is of course quite obvious that arrangements could be improved. It seems to some people that overseas service is just the same as home service when it comes to qualifications for getting out of the army – but the men who make these arrangements obviously have a lot to learn.

29 November 1944

Well darling, I certainly don't expect to get home for Xmas now but I wouldn't be at all surprised if something happened in the early spring. I came near to coming home early last spring, but of course I would have been in France now if I had come. Up to date I am as fit and healthy now as when I came into the army and somehow I feel that I could be in many worse places than here. I don't want to go to Burma. I'm not frightened of any Japs but I know the dangers of malaria and dysentery. All the time I am here (hundreds of miles behind the front) it is becoming more unlikely that I shall be sent there. But I want to come home and make love to my missus.

George was not lacking in physical courage but had a horror of dirt and disease, a horror which together with his love for Maud kept him away from the temptations of the flesh that the men were so often warned about, and helped to keep him remarkably healthy throughout the campaign.

3 December 1944

I am out with the band five nights each week. My fiddle came unstuck again through the damp weather – that's three times it has gone. One thing about the old band – it gets me out of guards and it keeps me busy all the time.

5 December 1944

There is a great excitement among several of the lads about this leave. I think perhaps I was wrong when I said there was a catch in it. It seems that the lads with the longest service up to four years, in each unit that gets an allocation, are the ones that go, and then they return to their unit to finish their overseas service, i.e. four and a half years. Well I think at least three of my mates will be home for Xmas. I stand a chance of getting home in the spring. In the meantime I must say that I am having the best time since I have been overseas.

There is one thing that doesn't seem quite right over this leave – some units have a lot more long service lads than others making it possible for one lad in one unit to go home while another lad with the same length of service, but in a different unit with more long service men, would have to wait.

8 December 1944

Many thanks for the dancing snaps that have arrived safely. I think they are good. You might tell our Jean that I think she is getting a pair of legs just like Betty Grable and our Julie is a lovely little girl. You know we are very lucky to have such beautiful children.

26. Jean in tap-dancing gear at the garden party, September 1944.

Jean's legs did not grow to compete with those of Betty Grable, but Julie was certainly the pretty one. The photos had been taken at a garden party back in the summer when pupils of the local dancing teacher had given a dancing display. Julie, the youngest of the performers – supple, vivacious and with a good sense of rhythm – had stolen the show with her performance as a thistledown fairy.

21 December 1944

We are playing on Christmas morning at the hospital where our saxophone and clarinet player is – he will be well enough to join in while he is in bed. Then I expect we shall have our Christmas dinner at about 2.30 and a do afterwards – but we are hoping to get the evening free. It's been a bit too much just lately – every night late nights and work throughout the day. But I think we shall have some different arrangement in the New Year.

I had the day off the other day and went to the opera and saw *Cavalleria Rusticana* and *I Pagliacci.* Unfortunately I had to leave before the latter was finished in order to get back as we had a job on.

The next letter was to his daughters:

24 December 1944

It has turned very cold. Daddy's pal Bill is busy chopping wood for our fire. We are chopping up everything we can find to keep us warm. Your Dad is going to play in a hospital tomorrow morning, where there are lots of wounded soldiers, and we shall do our best to make them happy.

There was nothing in George's letters that year about their Christmas dinner. Perhaps that was in a missing letter, or maybe he regarded that year's celebrations as a rather poor do. The war diary, however, records, 'Although Christmas Day was a normal working day the Unit contrived to foster the spirit of the season by decorating the billet, messrooms etc., and having a Social Evening after an excellent dinner. Unit dance band played in one of the wards of 100 General Hospital.'[7]

8 January 1945

We have only two band jobs on this week (we are having a rest period) and then next week we start again and it will be every night ... [but] you need not worry about me doing too much – I shan't. I've been in the army long enough now to know when and when not to take things easy.

We are having a meeting tonight and I think it is about leave. I think I know what it is all about but I'll let you know in my next letter. I'll tell you one thing though – 'Mister Grigg' isn't very popular among some of the lads. I think Hore-Belisha would have organised things more to our satisfaction.

The Rt Hon. Leslie Hore-Belisha had been secretary of state for war from 1937, but he left office in January 1940 and went on to become a powerful critic of Churchill's leadership when, in June 1940, it looked as if Alexandria would fall to Rommel's flaming sword.[8] In a surprise move, in 1942, Churchill had appointed Sir James Grigg, previously the permanent secretary in the War Office, to become secretary of state. It was Sir James whom George, understandably, blamed for the bizarre, inequitable and ever-changing leave arrangements. However, it is likely the army authorities were more to blame, for the details of their implementation rested with the local command.[9]

11 January 1945

Well darling here is some news about leave. First of all what they call the Python Scheme is in action for long service men overseas, and the period is 4½ years. Then they brought out this special leave of one month in the UK and then returning to complete long service, and the arrangement was for this leave to go to the men who had done between 3 and 4 years. Well now it has changed and apparently some of the men who haven't been out here so long feel they should be included in the home leave scheme, so now it is available for men who have done from 2 to 3½ years. You see what this means – all the men who have done 3½ or over are out of it and must wait another 12 months before they get a break.

For the remaining lads who have done 2 to 3½ years the priority *isn't* going to the men who have been out longest – it will be decided by chance i.e. drawing out of the hat. There are 28 originals who have done just on 3¼ years and it is very unlikely that more than 6 leave passes will be granted to us during the next 3 months, if that. It is possible that none of the 28 (and I am one of them) will get it under this 'system'.

So darling I have told you all I know ... [but] if I were forced to be apart for 20 years I would always be faithful and in love with my missus.

Any hopes that George and Bill might have had about home leave under the LIAP scheme were now dashed, and Bill must have been feeling doubly sore:

21 January 1945

Poor old Bill has a broken nose and two black eyes – he is always hurting himself. So I am making it as easy as possible for him. He should be alright in a day or two.

24 January 1945

I have just seen an announcement in the *Union Jack* that priority would go to good-conduct front-line men and long service. I'm all in favour of front-line men and injured and wounded men going first but it certainly isn't right for 2-year men to go home when 3½-year men cannot.

Although the men did not have access to a radio to hear the BBC's broadcasts to the troops, it seems that they were kept well-informed by the *Union Jack*, the newspaper for the British fighting forces. George's letter goes on to mention his pay rise. An extra tanner a day may not have been much of a consolation for being away from his family so long, but at least it made him financially far better off than he would be for many years after the war:

> I've had a tanner a day rise to celebrate my fourth anniversary. I get 6/6 a day of which 1/3 goes to you leaving me 5/3 a day clear ...

> *28 January 1945*
>
> I have made myself a bed with wood and canvas. For the last 12 months we have been sleeping on 3 planks resting on short trestles which was quite a good idea for we were moving about lot (they would be easier to carry on a wagon) but now we are allowed to make ourselves as comfy as possible.
>
> We are doing very well for grub these days – the food is much about the same, mostly dehydrated, but the cooks seem to have better methods of turning it out.

It is unclear why, when the officers were living in a block of flats in town, George and Bill were not allowed to make themselves comfortable by constructing permanent beds. Perhaps it had been assumed that the Eighth Army would make faster progress north and the depot would need to move. Or perhaps the men's tents and huts were frequently moved about the depot site as it expanded, or as an incoming commanding officer decided to reorganize it. Certainly the depot was huge, covering 3 square miles of open country, and it was operating as the main holding depot for petroleum products for western Italy. Records for the previous December show that it was handling an average of 1,500 tons of packed products per day, and dispatching supplies to centres as far apart as Brindisi on the south-east coast to Falconara Marittima, just north of Ancona on the north-east coast, as well as to Rome in the west (see map on page 96).[10]

> *30 January 1945*
>
> Yes Darling you have got the leave scheme right. If I don't come before I've completed 3½ years – well 'I've had it' and must do the full 4½ years before I see you. I think our best hopes lie in the Russians finishing off the war quickly.

George's pessimism was well-founded: he would have to wait until long after the Russians had helped end the war in Europe. Meanwhile he and Bill had to make the most of Italy – and they were good at that:

1 February 1945

I had the day off yesterday and in company with another lad we made our way to town and our first port of call was the Royal Palace where we had tea and cakes and listened to the band. There are some lovely paintings on show there both on the ceiling and in frames. One of them is a view of the bay with Nelson's fleet anchored near to the shore. It makes me think how much better it is now for the palace to benefit thousands of service men instead of, as in the days gone by, one man only or one man and the family and his hundreds of servants. Why don't they do the same with places like Buckingham Palace and other large buildings?

7 February 1945

Tomorrow I am going on 7 days leave to Rome with old Bill. They have only just told us and we have made quite sure that it won't affect our chance of home leave in any way. So we are going. It is a wonder that they are letting the two of us go at once but we have got two blokes to do the job. The last leave we had at Alex in August or September 1942 and then they would not let us go together. So we should have a good time.

9 February 1945

Yesterday morning Bill and I got up at 5.30 in the morning and had our break-fast and tied up our blankets and small kit and were taken to town by car driven by one of our mates where we were to pick up the leave party. Well we waited a long time and then got aboard a truck with 13 other lads and, after another wait, we got away. After being on the road for a short while the driver discovered that he needed petrol ... [then] his engine conked out and that meant a lot more waiting. When we got on the go again he could only do about 15 or 20 mph and the fumes from his engine nearly choked us. We should have got to Rome about 1 or 2 o'clock but instead it was 8 o'clock and quite dark, and then the driver didn't know where to go, and we wandered all over the place in a truck that kept breaking down. Once he nearly backed into the Tiber when trying to turn round. Well eventually we in the back got fed up – we got out and got on the phone ...

When we got to the rest camp, by a fluke, there was no one to receive us. It is a big place but it is new and they haven't really had time to get things perfectly organised. However, when the Colonel was accidentally aroused he well and truly shook everybody up, and we soon found the cookhouse and our beds. After something to eat I made my bed on the bottom of a double wooden bunk, and I crept into bed with a sigh of relief – then the damn bunk collapsed much to Bill's amusement.

But after this inauspicious start George and Bill had a fine time in Rome, and George sent home dozens of postcards.

10 February 1945

We were told that we must be present to hear an address by the Colonel at 14.00 hrs or we would miss our NAAFI ration. However, we had promised to meet our chief clerk and his mate, who are also on leave here, at the Victor Emmanuel monument – which we soon found. This is where old 'Musso' used to address the people from the balcony ... Well after wandering around ... we got back to the Rest Camp where we had a good lunch and heard the Colonel's address, which was a description of what we could do ending with the usual warning about the women.

In the town again we visited a fine old church and the coliseum which is a wonderful edifice. One thing that struck me very much is the lovely fur coats the young women wear and it is quite easy to understand why. To sleep for the night accompanied costs 25 dollars (£6.5.0). The people are certainly a lot better off here than further south. The buildings are beautiful and there are

27. The Coliseum: one of many postcards George sent home from Rome.

statues and monuments everywhere. I suppose the reason why the buildings are so clean is that very little coal is used.

Modern Rome is built on and around ancient Rome and you can see old relics and ruins mingling with new buildings. Some of the prized statues are partly bricked to prevent war damage, but Rome apparently hasn't seen anything of the war like poor old London. It is quite obvious that Rome has been visited by many American soldiers because the price of everything is fantastic. It is indeed fortunate that there is a good NAAFI.

We have done quite a lot of walking today – quite a change from a pair of skidding wheels.

A British officer in Rome, writing about a month later, noted how the influx of American servicemen had greatly inflated the cost of living:

In 1937, a reasonably good-looking tart would be valued at say 180 lire for the night. And dear at that. About 37/- at sterling rates then. The Yanks pay – the fools – up to 3,000 lire, or over £7 ... For every British officer there were ten Yanks, mostly very, very young and behaving as adolescents. They are mocked, swindled and despised by the Romans. The British are swindled and, I think, pitied. They cannot understand why Britain – to them a great power – does not pay its soldiers on the same level as the Yanks.[11]

But with the NAAFI to fall back on, our more mature privates were able to enjoy the less expensive pleasures of Rome:

14 February 1945

We have spent a lot of time in the Roman Forum where there are many of the really ancient buildings. Do you remember the Capitol where the geese quacked and saved the garrison? Old Bill took a snap of me up there, which I will be sending on.

On one occasion we climbed right up to the top of the dome [of St Peter's] and right into the bronze ball above it and we could see out of the little slits down and around. We could trace the seven hills of Rome, and the various outstanding buildings and the mountains in the distance. On another occasion we visited the Vatican City and had an audience with the Pope. He spoke to us in 'Itie' but whether he was blessing or cussing us I don't know.

22 February 1945

We've finished our Rome holiday and had a jolly good week there. We spent very little money – we didn't need it. When we had our food out we went to the NAAFI.

28. George and Bill in the Roman
Forum, February 1945.

29. Three soldiers in the Roman
Forum, February 1945.

The NAAFI in Rome, opened the previous summer, provided cheap food but it was more than a spartan canteen. It boasted cafeterias, snack bars, soda fountains, games rooms, music rooms, lounges, a gift shop, a library, a barber's shop, a photographer's, orchestras, cinemas and other amenities.[12] George's letter went on to talk of another treat:

> We did a great deal of walking ... [and] saw a wonderful performance of *Aida* by Verdi at the Opera House. It was the finest stage display I've ever seen with hundreds of people on at once. There were more than a hundred in the orchestra and the music was beautiful. A bloke named Gigli took the leading tenor part. I don't know if he was the Gigli but he had a fine voice.

The leading tenor could not have been *the* Gigli, Beniamino Gigli, who wowed audiences in Italy and London in the 1930s and was a favourite with Mussolini, for he was decidedly out of favour by this time. In fact, in 1944 the Allied military authorities had forbidden him to give public performances for fear of inciting disturbances. His banishment did not last long, however, and soon after the war he was again delighting audiences in Britain. The programme which George sent to Maud shows that in this lavish performance at the Royal Opera House it was Renato Gigli who sang the part of the hero, Radames, with the beautiful dramatic soprano Iva Pacetti in the role of Aida.

Meanwhile, back at the petrol depot, the pressure of work had not eased. British guards had taken over from the Italians, but the civilian labour had been nearly doubled to 810 people to meet the increasing workload. The depot, by now well behind the front, does not appear to have suffered from enemy attack but there was now concern about the possibility of damage by rioting civilians or sabotage. The army was anxious that any such disturbances should be left to the Italian authorities to deal with. The unit's diary noted: 'The responsibility of quelling civilian riots etc. is primarily that of the Italian admin authority and Italian and/or British troops will NOT be used unless authorised by 56 Area.'[13] George, too, was having to cope with a heavy workload:

28 February 1945

I am very busy just now. Old Bill has finished with the motor bike – it got on his nerves and he used to shout in his sleep, and so now he has gone on a wagon. I've another fellow in his place but he isn't much use. In fact from today he is away for four days. We are very busy with the old band too – we are out for the next seven nights.

4 March 1945

I've had a devil of a time, but it should get easier now as I've got the other bloke with me. I broke the frame of my bike travelling over rough roads so they got him back again. This morning I shall go out to a dump to look for parts.

Despite his bike breaking under him from time to time, George's letters never say anything about getting hurt himself. They give the impression that it was always the unfortunate Bill who became ill or had an accident. There was at least one occasion, however, when George was not quite so lucky. Years later he told his family about the time when, having struck a pothole, he was thrown off his bike and it burst into flames. Several Italian women ran over to him and, ignoring the danger, pulled him away from the burning bike, shouting, '*Ospedali!*' They stayed with him until they were sure he was on his way to the hospital, where he was well cared for by the nursing nuns.

16 March 1945

We had a dance on the night before last but through a mistake our saxophone and accordionist had the needle 3 times and it nearly laid them out and they didn't turn up. So there was only piano, drums and me on the fiddle – but we got on alright. During the interlude I played one or two solos and an Itie girl who had been watching my fiddle intently for some time suddenly bucked up courage and played a little solo on it quite well.

17 March 1945

Another late night last night. All the big bugs from around were there and we didn't think much of it. They tried to work us too hard – too many numbers without a break. Eventually we let them know what we thought. I doubt whether we shall go there again. Usually we get every consideration and expect to be treated as equals.

George never mentioned the rank of the other band members but, as musicians, they earned a respect that cut across the usual rigid hierarchy – so much so that, by this time, they expected to be treated as equals when they were performing.

24 March 1945

We have seen some Ities who have been in England and they say what a good time they had. One of them showed us his girl's photo. What a lark if it had been one of the missus – and what a dust up afterwards ... Old Bill and I had the day off yesterday but didn't do much except stroll around and go to the pictures. It won't be long before we take our bathing costumes for the sea already looks rather tempting.

Well darling the news is grand this morning and in Germany it is beginning to look very much like the last round up. That's my only chance of getting home now because no leave vacancies are coming through for any of us. We are losing some of our young mates who are going in the Infantry, but there isn't much chance of old Bill and I going in it. I wouldn't mind if it would make it any quicker for getting home.

The day before, British forces under Montgomery had crossed the Rhine in Northern Germany, enabling them to move into the Ruhr, the heart of the German weapons manufacturing industry. So perhaps it would not be so long before he would be able to talk to his wife. It had been three and a half years since Maud had heard her husband's voice:

2 April 1945

I hear that it is possible to have a recording of a message to send home and when I go to town today I shall find out about it. So perhaps before long you will hear your old man speaking to you.

4 April 1945

I made the record yesterday morning. It will go by air to London and will be posted on to you from there. I shall send another as soon as I can ... [but] at the moment they can only do 50 each day and the demand is much greater than the supply.

It appears that this time the recording did reach her, for among his letters, she had kept a tiny record labelled 'Voices of the Forces'. The shiny cardboard disc, about 5 inches across and warped with age, has a thin black coating incised with grooves, and in addition to the central hole for the pin of the turntable, there is another hole in the label with an instruction: 'Should the disc slip pin to turntable through hole in label.' Its arrival must have been at first thrilling but then, almost certainly, a disappointment. Maud wrote 'not very good' on the envelope. It was too small to play on Jean's more recently acquired record player, so George's voice remains locked away within that flimsy disc. The letter continued:

We get free tickets to see the latest Yankee films, that is because there is no other form of entertainment around here. There are no nice walks nearby either, because every bit of ground is under cultivation – some of it stinks too because of the manure they use. They go round the latrines, lower a bucket on a rope and haul it up and empty it into a large barrel mounted on two wheels drawn by a horse. You can smell them coming from a long way off.

There are no further letters from George in April – the month that saw the enemy crumble. The remnants of the Eighth Army, which had maintained a war of attrition against the entrenched German forces throughout the cold rain and snow of the Italian winter, launched a major offensive when the weather improved. They broke through into the Po Valley in early April 1945, and on 29 April the German forces in Italy surrendered unconditionally to Alexander, by now Field Marshal Alexander. The day before, Mussolini and his mistress were shot and their bodies displayed upside down in Milan. On 30 April, Hitler killed himself and the mistress he had married the day before. The German forces in north-west Germany surrendered to Montgomery on 4 May and three days later Germany signed the unconditional surrender at Eisenhower's headquarters. The instrument was ratified by the Russians the following day and so, 'in a final stroke of muddle' the western Allies celebrate VE Day (Victory in Europe) on 7 May and the Russians on 8 May.[14]

Maud kept the dog-eared leaflet in which Field Marshal Alexander expressed his fulsome thanks to the 'Soldiers, Sailors and Airmen of the Allied Forces in the Mediterranean Theatre':

You have won a victory which has ended in the complete and utter rout of the German armed forces in the Mediterranean. By clearing Italy of the last Nazi aggressor, you have liberated a country of over 40,000 people.

Today the remnants of a once proud Army have laid down their arms to you – close on a million men with all their arms, equipment and impediments.

No praise is high enough for you sailors, solders, airmen and workers of the United Forces in Italy for your magnificent triumph.

My gratitude to you and my admiration is unbounded and only equalled by the pride which is mine in being your Commander-in-Chief.

George's comments were more laconic:

7 May 1945

Well Darlings it's as good as over in Europe now and VE Day may be officially declared before you get this. I expect we shall have to stay in camp because some of the lads might get too merry ... I can't really say that I am greatly excited over the news. I've got a feeling that there are many more troubles to face somehow. I haven't got any idea when I might be coming home. There are still men out here who have done well over four years and they don't know.

8 May 1945

We had a bit of a celebration last night. I didn't get drunk but I've got a thick head. Today is a normal working day – up at 6 o'clock – but tomorrow is to be our official VE Day ...

12 May 1945

This will have to be a quick one as I have been ever so busy this week. The other bloke who is supposed to help is useless, and dodges all he can. But we had the day off last Wednesday to celebrate VE Day. We played football in the morning and in the afternoon we had a dance in a big stone barn in the Depot. There were lots of women, some in their working clothes, so it was something like an old-fashioned peasants' barn dance. I must have been on form because I was never short of vermouth from the lads who seemed to appreciate my fiddling. It was very warm and the sweat was rolling off us. After tea there were free drinks in the canteen – no beer, only vermouth. That stuff makes them fight, and they did. The joint was just about wrecked and some of them had to be carried out.

Although the fighting in the Far East continued, the official fighting in Europe was over. However, George was not alone in feeling that, despite the euphoria of VE Day, there were many more troubles to come.

8

On the Dole in Castellammare

As George was well aware, victory in Europe did not mean that his army days would be over. But although he did not expect an early end to the fighting in the Far East, his hopes of getting some home leave appear to have been revived:

> *15 May 1945*
>
> I think that they will keep me in the army for another 12 months but I should get home on leave sometime this year. In the meantime things are going on just the same. We have the same routine and work to do. Under the Yankee points system I would be wearing civvies now. Sir James Grigg said once that when the war with Germany was over all the 3-year men and over would go home. Now we must wait and see what happens.

The US Army, it seems, gave priority to married men with children; the British system remained, at least in its execution, more arbitrary and inequitable. It was frustrating, but for George and Bill there could have been worse places to be waiting than in Southern Italy in the summer:

> *16 May 1945*
>
> Last night we got on a lorry and off we went down to the sea and had our first swim this year and it was grand. We shall have a lorry laid on to take a swimming party two or three times a week. I thought of you when I was in the water and I know you would have loved it. It was warm in some places and cold in others.

> *21 May 1945*
>
> We played in a concert last night in a newly built concert hall. After the show the colonel introduced me to a pal of his, 'Johnnie Walker', and we had a bit of

a singsong. Tonight I am going to the opera. Gigli is taking the leading part in *Manon Lescaut*.

28 May 1945

We are playing in a dance band competition on Sunday next in a large theatre – like an opera house with rows of boxes up and around. The finals will be played in the Palace to dancing, but I don't suppose we shall get there. The saxophone and clarinet players are very good – both in modern swing rhythm and quality of the melody. The piano player is a rough jewel – can't read a note of music and plays quite a number of wrong notes but seems to get away with it. However, he has a very good sense of dance rhythm. The drummer is good until he goes on the vermouth, which is often, and then sometimes he is too loud. The accordion player is rather weak. I'm alright on the waltzes and slow foxtrots but I've got a lot to learn with quicksteps especially when it comes to improvisation. You sort of have to have dance music in your blood to do it well. If I have a drop of beer or a tot of whisky I'm alright.

George would not have needed a tot of whisky to feel at home playing in a symphony orchestra or chamber music group, for his musical soul was firmly rooted in the classical German repertoire. He was happiest playing Beethoven sonatas or unaccompanied Bach, which he performed with a mellow tone and lyrical phrasing, but he also liked to have a go at the more flamboyant virtuoso works of Paganini or Sarasate. And it was not only on the fiddle that he enjoyed showing off, but on the sports field, too:

1 June 1945

We had a sports day this afternoon and all the lads turned out for it. I went in the Old Crocks as they called it for men over 35 – some of them were still 34 – and I won that. It was 100 yards and I was in quicker time than the open 100 yards. I was surprised as there were some fine built men in it. I got a 100-lire prize to use in the canteen. Some of the blokes said I ran so fast I don't need a motorbike.

The war diary recorded this event as taking place in 'Sandown Park' in Casoria and mentioned that George also competed in the high jump, and that he and Bill, inseparable for so long, ran together in the three-legged race.[1]

4 June 1945

We had the band contest last night and got knocked out, but our saxophone and clarinet players got the individual instrument prizes. There were some first-class bands with more and better instruments than we had. Our blokes said we put up quite a good show but I think we might had done better if we had properly arranged numbers for our combination – but the pianist and drummer don't know anything about reading music and the accordionist very little. I wished I had my own fiddle with me but I did the best I could out of the one I'd got – it isn't much good and breaks in half every so often. I told them that if it broke while I was on the job I should sing the rest ...

The band had been struggling for a long time to acquire new instruments or to get their old ones repaired. The problem eventually became recognised officially. An entry in the war diary the previous month recorded that the dance band, which had been performing for over 3½ years and was now doing so four evenings a week, was in danger of having to stop playing as its instruments were wearing out. It noted, 'All these instruments, with the exception of the piano, are the original ones bought in the UK and, although they have been used almost continuously since then, have had no major repairs. The present cost of repairs/ or new instruments, is quite beyond the resources of this small band.' The unit put in an official request for pads for a saxophone, clarinet reeds, accordion bellows, new skins for drums, and cymbals, and for the violin bow to be re-haired.[2]

Years later George talked about the day when he persuaded Bill to help him get some hairs to re-hair his bow. The plan was for him to keep the horse still and happy by stroking its muzzle, while Bill would nip behind to cut some hairs from its tail. According to this version of the story, the horse kicked Bill and bolted before he could get any hair. Bill sent home several photos of George with a horse; perhaps that was the horse that kicked Bill – or could it have been George who came off worse this time? We shall never know.

10 June 1945

I am having quite a full life these days – plenty of work and more play than usual. I played cricket the other evening and caught three blokes out. When I went in I slashed out at everything and caught one a beauty and sent it to the boundary, but I put so much effort into it that I went spinning round and landed on my backside.

Whether battling at cricket, running races or swimming in the sea, George threw himself into such activities with gusto, and clearly enjoyed demonstrating his prowess. But the inequities and uncertainties of the leave arrangements continued to dominate his letters:

I expect you know that Python has been reduced to 4 years. I doubt whether they will give me leave now. The completion of my four years overseas will be very near my demobilisation date so it wouldn't surprise me in the least

30. Was this the uncooperative horse?

if they don't arrange the two together – that would deprive me of a month's holiday. Some of the lads are lucky like Bill Bailey – he went home at Xmas on leave for a month and now he has gone home on Python. Of course I'm voting Socialist.

14 June 1945

Did you read about what old Grigg had to say about leave? Although Python is supposed to be reduced to 4 years, but I think it will take some time for that to really take effect since I know more than one bloke who has done 4½ and is still wondering when his time will come. Possibly that might have something to do with election. Grigg said the 7,500 men a day were going home on leave from BLA[3] but only 2,000 a month from Italy etc. I think he also as good as admitted that the LIAP had been a mistake, as it had raised too many hopes and expectations amongst the men and more especially the wives. He said that some wives had accused their husbands of deliberately prolonging their stay out here. Of course it was a mistake, and what few leaves were granted should have been for the Python men or for compassionate leave.

In his statement to the House of Commons on 8 June, Sir James had acknowledged that only a small number of men had been granted leave under LIAP and that, inevitably, by running the two schemes together, some anomalies in allocation were bound to occur. However, he assured the House that troops from Italy and the BLA would be sent home as soon as transport became available. Shipping remained a problem and, on the overland route, bridges had been blown up and rolling stock was in short supply. But he promised 'all being well, to make a beginning by using road transport this month and heavy bombers next month'.[4]

19 June 1945

I'm sorry my letters just lately have upset you – perhaps I have been too pessimistic. Perhaps public opinion in England might cause them to hurry up ...

When I really do get home my big ambition is to make my Maudie, Jean and Julie as happy as possible. I've seen such a lot of what is bad, and the kind of life which some people like to lead which sickens me, that I long to be with my little family.

24 June 1945

I am sending home all the things that I don't need. I have packed up the banjo that I bought in Sicily for the kids to play with.

4 July 1945

We went swimming yesterday afternoon and the sea was rough and the rest of the boys were a bit nervous – even the better swimmers – and stayed right close to the shore. But I got fed up with that and went out for a long swim and it was grand, just like being in another world with the sun streaming down on the surf. I am still doing a fair amount of work even though the war is over but we are getting quite a few breaks for swimming ...

There is quite a strong labour movement among the lads here – if the people at home are anything like us old Attlee should get a good backing.

The General Election took place the next day, but the results were not declared for another three weeks to enable the votes of the overseas forces to be returned and counted. Whatever trust George might have had in the wisdom of the establishment before he joined up – probably not very much – the inequities of the leave arrangements, and delays in implementation, confirmed that a radical change was needed. The educational discussions organised by the ABCA, which

IV. ABCA: Education or Subversion?

The Army Bureau of Current Affairs was the brainchild of W. E. Williams, who became its director in 1941. Williams, who had been chief editor of Penguin Books before the war and went on to be secretary general of the Arts Council afterwards, felt passionately that the 'fighting men and women had a right to basic factual information, to political curiosity, and to a feeling of partnership in deciding what kind of a country Britain should be after the War had been won'.[5]

The bureau issued fortnightly bulletins to brief officers on topics of current interest. It also published a series of pamphlets, entitled *The British Way of Life*, covering such subjects as social security policy, educational planning, trade unionism and local government. Designated officers were trained to introduce the subjects and to encourage the men to discuss the issues, uninhibited by rank. Richard Hoggart, who came across the bureau's work in Naples, described the pamphlets as 'models of exposition for adults who had little background to the issues they treated but were assumed to be intelligent enough to grasp an argument clearly presented. They did not talk down, and underestimated neither the subject nor the capacity of the readers ... They were factual, concise, and entirely without the chauvinistic blarney which disfigured so much in official handouts.'[6] The standard of the discussion sessions, based on the pamphlets, was another matter. Leslie Wayper, in his history of army education, suggests they were patchy in execution, sometimes ill-presented by the unit officer, and resented by the men.[7]

Hoggart, while accepting that the intended clarity of the pamphlets may have become blurred by the presentation, argued that they introduced the men not only to a wide range of subjects but also 'to the idea that they could have, should have, a say in the discussion and resolution of them'. [8] Not surprisingly, therefore, they did not always meet with official approval. The pamphlet on the Beveridge Plan, written by Beveridge himself, was withdrawn following government concerns about the financial implications of his proposals. Nor were the authorities happy when, in January 1944, a discussion session in Cairo evolved into a mock election which overwhelmingly returned a Labour Government. Goebbels interpreted this as mutiny in the British Army, and it brought to an end the military career of the officer who ran the event.[9]

George and his mates attended, may also have helped to influence the way they voted. Richard Hoggart, who was involved in educational activities for the forces in Naples, suggested that the ABCA's pamphlets and the regular talks and discussion sessions based on them all over the world did a great deal to make many soldiers vote for Attlee 'not because ABCA's activities were barely disguised socialist propaganda (they were not), but because they helped reduce the power of the mandarin voices, accelerated decline in deference, made soldiers realize they did have a right to think for themselves'.[10] The forces' vote was too small to have a significant effect on the outcome, but it did contribute to Attlee's resounding victory.

The men of No. 8 Petrol Depot were now redundant, for on 1 July the No. 130 Petrol Depot of the RASC took over responsibility for all operations at the Casoria depot. The war diary mentions that a recreational training programme was set up for the men while they awaited instructions to move.

7 July 1945

I see the *Queen Mary, Queen Elizabeth* and *Aquitania* are very busy taking Yanks home. Hundreds of Yanks are going to Paris by plane from an airfield near where we are. I make no comment – what's the use.

As the Americans were being flown home from the airfield just a couple of miles away, the men from the petrol depot had to console themselves with some organised sightseeing trips to Monte Cassino, Vesuvius, Pompeii and Solfatara. There is no record of George visiting Cassino – perhaps he was none too keen to see another scene of recent devastation – but he was enthralled by Pompeii and intrigued by Solfatara, where an old man showed them round the extinct volcano with holes and cracks exuding steam and sulphurous gases. But the climb up Vesuvius was the most fun.

11 July 1945

The first part was beautiful where there was vegetation on the hillsides – there were tons of peaches, tomatoes, plums and grapes growing, in fact some of the villagers pelted us with peaches as we went by in the truck. The road was so narrow that our truck had a job to get round some of the bends and we couldn't go up the road (or lane) all the way because the last lot of lava had cut across it ... When we had taken the truck up as far as we could, a guide met us and gave us each a stick in exchange for a fag and off we started. I was in the front of the single file of lads, just behind the guide, because I guessed there would be a lot of dust and I was right ... the guide was telling us how many observation stations had been swallowed up ... The crater was very strange

31. George and Bill by the sea at Torre Annunziata, July 1945.

– no boiling lava but the gases kept blowing up the stones like bubbles and the heat was intense. The sides were steaming and crumbling and rocks kept on falling down. It is 300 feet deep and several hundred across. We went half way round the rim and back again. I made up my mind that if I did slip it wouldn't be inside.

On the way down we had a wild slide down the slope and couldn't stop ourselves and we got smothered in dust. Afterwards I found that my boots needed repairing.

18 July 1945

I told you that another leave had been granted to this unit which went to a 2-year man. Well he is on his way ... [but] we have men who have done nearly 4½ years who are aching their hearts away to get home. I have been patient all these years but now it is getting a bit too much. If we were doing a useful job of work it would be easier.

19 July 1945

You say Jean has missed a lot of schooling and Julie had thin white legs. Have they been ill? I want the truth you know.

George and Maud had agreed to tell each other their bad news as well as the good but, of course, that was a promise neither of them could keep. Maud occasionally mentioned the children's colds and minor ailments, after they had recovered, but she had not told George about Jean's more serious illnesses that kept her away from school throughout much of 1943 and 1944. She had not told him when, in the previous year, Jean had been critically ill with pneumonia. At that time it was not uncommon for children to die from common illnesses such as measles and whooping cough. Jean had them all, and then succumbed to pneumonia. That same winter, one of her school friends living in the next street died from pneumonia and, many years before, it was pneumonia that had killed Maud's first fiancé. Maud was sick with fear, a fear that she could not share with George. But Jean was lucky. Unlike her schoolfriend, who had been left to fend for herself during the daytime, Jean had a grandmother to care for her during the day, and a mother to watch over her at night. But it was probably the white tablets imprinted with 'M&B' and smothered in jam to make them palatable – the newly introduced wonder-drug penicillin – that saved her, and enabled her to make the first wobbly steps across the bedroom.

At one point Maud asked the doctor what on earth she could do to improve the health of her chronically sick daughter, at which he asked, 'Where does she come from?' On hearing that it was Eastbourne, he replied, 'Take her back there.' Now, with the war in Europe over, she could do just that. In July 1945 Maud and the two girls returned to Eastbourne for a holiday, and stayed at her mother's house. While Jean and Julie were left to enjoy long blissful days on the beach – making sandcastles and pools when the tide was low and trying to swim when it was high – Maud set about finding a house for them to live in.

While the carpet gardens on the seafront were blooming again and the military bands played to sunburnt faces in deckchairs, the town just behind was punctured with bombsites and derelict buildings. Maud was particularly saddened to find that the Technical Institute, where she had enjoyed evening classes, was no long standing. But the shortage of council housing, as in the country generally, was of more immediate concern. Each day Maud assailed the housing department. On a second visit, some months later, she finally persuaded them that she could afford to pay the rent on a council house. She needed to be forceful and persuasive, for the rent was 25/- a week and although she received a relatively generous allowance of £3 a week as an army wife, this would soon stop and George's future income was uncertain.[11] While he was wondering about emigrating to a sunnier land, Maud had no doubts about where she wanted to live; she was determined to secure a house in her home town, close to the sea and the downs. The new home – to which they would now soon be moving – was an end-of-terrace house, requisitioned earlier in the war and much knocked about by the troops that had been billeted there, but it had a tiny garden and, best of all, it was only a few minutes walk from the sea.

32. Eastbourne's grand Technical Institute, before its destruction in 1943.

For a few more months Maud and the children remained living in Rushden. Meanwhile George had moved to a very different seaside town on a spectacularly beautiful stretch of coast.

1 August 1945

Here we are in the middle of a seaside town in a large building. I look out of the windows (or rather the openings as there aren't any windows) and wooded mountains tower up towards the sky, and then on the other side is the blue sea. We are sort of on the dole now. I am still on the bike doing routine jobs like fetching the mail but the others are just mucking around or on fatiguing, spud-bashing etc. ... We are all in one room with another mob. Gawd knows what they'll do with us.

Although his letters home no longer had to declare on the outside, 'I certify on my honour that the contents of this envelope refer to nothing but private and family matters,' and be signed by the writer, George still refrained, presumably from habit, from stating where he was. They were in fact in Castellammare di Stabia on the northern coast of the Sorrento Peninsula, overlooking the Gulf of Naples, which, before the war, was described as 'a favourable summer resort on account of its mineral waters (impregnated with sulphur and carbonic acid gas and partly radio-active, beneficial in cases of gout, intestinal disorder, etc.)'.[12] The unit had moved there on 1 August and was now, again, awaiting further instructions. Castellammare was a more enjoyable location than Casoria for a sea-loving man. In a letter to his two daughters, George described one good sea day when he had another chance to show off his physical skills:

3 August 1945

In the afternoon we all went off for a swim. We found a lovely place where the wooded mountains drop down to the calm blue sea. First of all Dad swam out to where a diving raft was moored in deep water and then swam back to the beach where he had a sun bathe ... Well then one of the soldiers had a board which he tied to our motor-boat with a long piece of rope, stood up on it and did some surf-riding. However, he tried to be clever and fell off. Three more soldiers tried and they fell off at once. So then Daddy dived off the boat and got on the board and off we went. It was thrilling – dancing up and down on the foam coming from the back of the boat. Daddy made the board swing from one side to the other and got on quite well but once he tried to be too clever and fell sideways, but he kept hold of the rope and somehow managed to roll onto the board and keep it balanced until he had the wind to stand up again.

6 August 1945

Grand news today – all our lads who have done over 4 years will be off this week. Perhaps I will be home next month. It's only an 8-hour trip by plane.

11 August 1945

The previous night was a very strange one. It was ever so close and hot and yet a strong wind was blowing in powerful gusts. The Ities said that Vesuvius was rumbling. It has been sort of dead this last few days and that is a sign that there is the possibility of an earthquake. While it is blowing off steam there is no danger because it is like a safety vent. The sea was calm in spite of the strong winds because it was blowing from the land and from the south. We couldn't sleep a wink all night and we were smothered in sweat. The next day the sea was rough and no swimming was allowed.

Castellammare di Stabia takes its name from its ninth-century castle, and from the remains of the ancient Roman town of Stabiae nearby. Stabiae, although a little further from Vesuvius than Pompeii, was also destroyed in the great eruption of AD 79, when it was engulfed in a thick layer of volcanic ash. The citizens of Castellammare had good reason to watch Vesuvius warily and listen to its rumblings. George's letter also alluded to more significant news:

Well the news sounds good – the Japs look like packing in as soon as they can.

As the war in Europe had been drawing to a conclusion, the war in the Far East intensified. Towards the end of 1944 American planes had begun the wholesale bombing of Japanese cities. Many of the bombs were incendiary devices, which turned the lightweight flammable buildings into raging infernos. By early August 1945 over sixty Japanese cities had been heavily bombed and about 600,000 people killed.[13] Then on 4 August, the first atom bomb was dropped on Hiroshima and a second fell on Nagasaki five days later, bringing unimaginable devastation and suffering. The bombs would, indeed, end the war – although it is by no means clear that the war would not have ended anyway.

But George, far from these horrors, was making the most of a summer by the sea. In another long letter to his daughters, he described a sailing trip that appears to have taken him around the Sorrento Peninsula and along the dramatic Amalfi Coast.

11 August 1945

We drove down to the dock in a truck and jumped off, and there she was moored by the quayside – a sailing schooner with an auxiliary engine (for when she has to go against the wind). We had to walk over a long narrow plank and if we had slipped we would have fallen into the sea, but we all managed it safely. Then Daddy, Uncle Bill and two other soldiers weighed the anchor and lashed it to the side of our ship. Our captain started up the engine and off we went, out of the harbour and into the open sea. Your old Dad climbed up to the bow of the schooner and held onto a cable with the sea directly beneath him and on either side. We all had our shirts off and looked like a bunch of pirates or a crowd of happy school boys.

Out into the sea our schooner rolled and tossed about just like a barrel and some of Daddy's pals soon began to have very pale faces, including Uncle Bill, but Dad was alright and thoroughly enjoying the voyage. After heading out to sea for some distance we turned in towards the coast where the mountains drop right down to the water and we went very close to the rocks, but there was no fear of us grounding because the sea was very deep. The scenery was exquisitely beautiful and changing continually as we sailed round various headlands. Sometimes we saw big caves but our schooner was too big to go exploring into them.

By the time we landed at a little harbour some of the soldiers were feeling very ill. They were very glad to be on dry land again, but Daddy enjoyed it all. We left our schooner and climbed up lots of steps and steep winding roads until we reached a town where we had tea, cakes and ice cream – and that promptly made one or two of the soldiers ill again.

Our schooner was waiting for us at the little harbour, but nothing would induce them to go back to it. No, they said they would rather walk home. Well, fortunately your Dad had been there before on his motorbike and knew the road home, so we all made our way off together … [but] a truck came along and picked us up, otherwise we might have been walking still.

Three days later, on 14 August, the Japanese Government accepted the terms of unconditional surrender and the next day was designated VJ Day. While his family in Rushden was enjoying a street party and dancing in the street, George's day was less fun:

15 August 1945

By way of celebrating VJ Day, Old Bill and myself are on a CMP charge.[14] I was just off on a run and met old Bill who was on his way back from the MOS for treatment, and just off from a 24-hour guard, and he was right browned off. So I got him to come with me on the back of my bike. Well we hadn't gone far when two MPs stopped us and put the pair of us on a charge: me for carrying a passenger not wearing a crash helmet, and Bill for riding on the back without a crash helmet. I knew the pillion passenger should wear a crash helmet but I have carried dozens of passengers not wearing helmets and have been seen by MPs on many occasions while doing so, but I have never been warned or told about it once. I most certainly did not know that one could be put on a charge for it. In our experience a CMP charge is a cut and dried affair so we are bound to get something – couple of weeks pay stopped I suppose. This will be the first in 4½ years – all the time in the army I've never had as much as two days CB.[15]

George and Bill got off lightly with a reprimand. Bill sent home a copy of the depot's newsletter which reported that 'Evans and Warner were pinched by the Red Caps the other day … They came up next day and were admonished. Said Warner in his insurance voice – "Thank you very much, Sir." – presumably for allowing him to stay on his money making job.' (This must be a reference to his role in the band.) The same newsletter gave warning of the return of the commanding officer who had issued such precise orders about stencilling crates. It noted, 'Needham is back with us but at present is out of harm's way on attachment …'

18 August 1945

Old Bill and I have written to the *Union Jack* with the suggestion that all experienced drivers with the longest service might be allowed to drive some of the surplus vehicles as far as the channel ports instead of leaving them for the Ities.

23 August 1945

The lads who have done just under 4 years are going into Lammie – that's the concentration camp for the lads going home. All I hope now is that they get good flying weather. They don't take off unless the weather is OK because there is no room to carry parachutes in the event of trouble and, of course, the journey is now non-stop. So with good weather they will clear them out faster and our turn will come sooner.

Lammie was a huge transit camp in Naples, built by the Royal Engineers to accommodate 5,000 personnel. It even had a swimming pool. But rather than await his transfer to Lammie, George longed to jump on his bike, with Bill on the back, and just keep driving north. However, there was a mountain to be climbed, and his letter continued:

Last evening Old Bill and I set off after tea and followed a short cut, which I had discovered on the bike, up into the mountains. We didn't have the time to climb the one we wanted and still get back in the light. We had passed a little village, dirty beyond description, where some of the males didn't appear to be too friendly, and when we found that we couldn't reach the top we decided to make our way back down a gorge. It was alright for the start and then there were several steep drops where we had to make detours. I kept on thinking to myself – by golly I've got to be careful now I've only got a very few weeks to go. Sometimes we made our way along the dry rocky bed, with steep cliffs on either side, but eventually we got down to the road.

3 September 1945

Everybody seems to have gone home bar us. The flies are awful here, the worst since living in Egypt and I've had several tummy aches through them getting on the grub. The old petrol depot was a first-class outfit for hygiene and sanitary purposes.

I will write telling you when I go into Lammie, but I might be home before you get the news. When I get to England I suppose I could send you a wire or perhaps phone – has Mrs Lord still got a phone and if so what is the number?

Mrs Lord, who lived diagonally opposite, was considerably better off than most of her neighbours and was one of the few people in the area to have a telephone. Before that letter could have reached Maud, however, he wrote another to Jean and Julie with even better news:

7 September 1945

It is quite likely that your old Dad will be home in a few days time – perhaps next week – in fact any time after you get this and indeed perhaps before. Dad will be flying home in a big bomber. Any morning at about 10 o'clock our plane

will take off and we shall arrive in about 4 o'clock in the afternoon. But he
doesn't know where it will land ...

In later years Maud's recollection was that George arrived home in early 1946,
but his army pay book shows that although he was not demobbed until 29 March
1946, he was given thirty-three days disembarkation leave on 14 September and
it was, presumably, on that day that he flew home with several other men, all
crowded together on the floor of a bomber with instructions not to move for
fear of upsetting the balance of the plane. Bill was not among that party. His
daughter recalls that he had to wait until the following January before he managed to get home. George's plane landed at an airfield not far from Rushden,
where Maud and the children were still living, but he couldn't get off there and
he had to continue on to another airfield further north. When he finally arrived
late one evening at Rushden's dimly lit railway station, Maud nearly threw her
arms around the wrong man. It was, after all, over four years since they had
seen, or talked to, each other. Fortunately George recognised Maud.

The following morning Jean woke to find a man in her mother's bed. As he
got out to hug her she noticed his rough suntanned skin, receding hair and missing front tooth. This was her long-awaited Daddy, a stranger – a not entirely
welcome stranger.

Coda

The Second World War was over but the devastation and suffering would linger on. Around 55 million people had been killed; 13 million children were left without parents; countless numbers would have to live with physical or psychological wounds; others had lost their loved ones, their homes or their livelihoods.[1] George and Bill were among the lucky ones.

There may have been horrors that George kept from his beloved 'Maudie', but he came home apparently unscathed, apart from his violin-playing hands, which had suffered from the vibrations of constant rough riding on his motorbike. The pale, slim young man who enlisted in 1941 came back a robust, middle-aged one – strengthened, both physically and psychologically, by those tough years abroad. He came back to a town, scarred by bombing, to find his insurance book severely depleted, but he was still determined to remain his own boss. For several years, to make ends meet, George and Maud ignored the council's rules and took in summer guests. Their visitors, many of them friends of Grandma from Rushden, enjoyed full board for three guineas a week. But it was hard work: carrying jugs of hot water up in the morning for there was only one tap in the house, boiling up sheets and towels in the copper for there was no washing machine, cooking meals three times a day while rationing was still in place. When the house was full, the family slept downstairs – George and Maud on a single divan-bed minus its mattress, Jean on the mattress on the floor, and Julie on an upturned rubber dingy.

George's skills at making do came in handy in peacetime. He grew as much food as possible in the tiny back garden – fertilized by the steaming droppings left by the horses in the road outside and with a miniature irrigation system inspired by the orchards of Sicily. He sawed up the driftwood that the family collected for the fire in lieu of coal and devised an extending brush to sweep the chimney. On one occasion he had to climb up on the roof to retrieve the brush, which had become detached and bloomed, like a black sunflower, in the chimney pot. He mended the family's shoes and made the children toys: a tiny sailing boat to sail on the pond in the park and a cricket bat and stumps for family cricket matches in the park or on the sands.

As his own boss, George could make sure that there was time for the important things in life: his family, his music, and long days in the sea and on the downs. He taught Julie, who inherited his good ear, to play the violin and somehow found the money for Jean to have lessons with the best piano teacher in town, lessons that were increasingly subsidised as the fees increased. The three of them enjoyed many a winter's evening making music together. In the summer, with homework and music practice done, they would all be out for a swim or a walk on the downs. With the help of friends, local building workers at the Artisans' Sailing Club, George and Maud made a sailing boat, and from then on sailing and racing were added to swimming as their summer passions. Every letter in those years abroad had repeated George's longing to return to his wife and young family, and his overriding concern to keep himself safe and fit for the 'real' life that lay ahead. He meant it. His life was totally devoted to his wife and family. Not for him an evening in the pub with his mates; he had no mates, nor any other social involvements. He lived for his family.

In his letters George had often talked of taking them to explore the mountains and lakes of Wales and Scotland, and to swim in the warm seas he had so enjoyed in Sicily and mainland Italy. Bill had returned to his family in South Wales and, although their friendship had been so close and supportive, George and Bill never met again. While their children were growing up, there was no money for such travel. By the early 1960s, however, with George's insurance book recovered and his daughters financially independent, he and Maud had a bit more money in their pockets, and they began to fulfil his dreams of exploring again. Taking their cue from Jean's hitchhiking journeys, they decided to hitch to Spain to explore the still-unspoilt capes and bays of the Costa Brava. The next time, they hitchhiked to Vienna and took, in addition to a small tent, formal evening dress so that they would be suitably attired for concerts there. It looked as if they were on the verge of a new freedom. Another expedition was planned for Italy, but that was not to be. George was diagnosed with advanced bowel cancer. After a long and very painful decline, he died at the age of fifty-five – just before his first grandchild was born. Could it have been the long-delayed result of army life, perhaps something as simple as brewing up tea in jerricans? Could it have been, after all those unheroic but stoical years, his army service that eventually killed him?

Bill, despite his many injuries and illnesses, lived on into his eighties in reasonably good health. He had no more trouble with his ear after, back home, a remnant of wartime bandage was found and removed. Some years after George's death, Gus moved into Maud's life. He taught her to paint and remained her companion, and eventually her carer, for the rest of her life – and it was a long one. Maud, having always hated that name, decided to call herself Jane. In the year that she turned 100, Gus and Jane held a joint exhibition of their art. She continued to paint, and to walk each day on the downs near Beachy Head, until the summer after her 102nd birthday. Later that year, when a leg infection meant she could no longer walk on the downs and breathe the sea air, she died.

Notes and References

1. Stumbling into War

1. Aspden 1978: 36.
2. Calder 1969: 57.
3. Aspden 1978: 42.
4. Stevens 1987: 28.
5. Aspden 1978: 42.
6. The report by the International Labour Office 1942: 117 confirms that initially cheese was too scarce to ration. The cheese ration fluctuated during the following years between 1 and 4 oz a week (Gardiner 2000: 120).
7. When the ultimatum to Germany expired at 11 a.m. on 3 September 1939, Britain was at war and this automatically included India and the colonies. The dominions were free to decide for themselves. Australia and New Zealand declared war straight away, without consulting their respective parliaments; South Africa and Canada followed after consultation (Taylor 1965: 452–3).
8. Wayper 2004: 167.
9. NA, WO 169/5881, 9 January 1942. (This and similar references are to the WO file series in the National Archives – Public Record Office.)

2. Skidding in the Sand

1. This assessment was made in May 1940 by General Wavell, commander-in-chief in the Middle East from 1939 to 1941, and quoted in Jackson 1975: 15.

2. RASC 1955: 108–11.
3. Baedeker 1929: 29.
4. Stocktaking ref. S/8ED/5, NA, WO 169/5881, 9 March 1942.
5. Dr Lutfallah, Professor of Graeco Roman History, quoted in Sattin 2000: 24–5.
6. Payton-Smith 1971: 239–42.
7. Ibid.: 353.
8. Thwaite 1969: 296.
9. Stocktaking ref. S/8ED/5, NA, WO 169/5881, 9 March 1942.
10. John Saintsbury, *http://www.wartimememories.co.uk/egypt.html*, accessed January 2010.
11. Flower and Reeves 1960: 243.
12. Churchill 1989: 590.
13. Williams 1963: 79–80.
14. Churchill 1989: 569.
15. NA, WO 169/5881, 13–14 July 1942.
16. Whiting 1987: 87.
17. Information from *http:touregypt.net/Desert.htm*, accessed August 2006.
18. Whiting 1987: 87.
19. Cigarettes, although not rationed, were usually scarce; clothing was rationed from July 1941, and soap from February 1942 (Gardiner 2000: 161 and 188).
20. Churchill 1989: 527.
21. S/SPD/18 in NA, WO 169/5881, 28 July 1942.

3. PT and Progress

1. Montgomery 1958: 100.
2. Ibid.: 99–101.
3. Churchill 1989: 614.
4. Montgomery 1958: 105.
5. Churchill 1989: 603.
6. Montgomery 1958: 84.
7. Ibid.: 123.
8. Flower and Reeves 1960: 458.
9. NA, WO 169/5881, August–September 1942.
10. Moorhead 1973: 154.
11. Hansard, House of Commons, 11 February 1943, col. 1462.
12. Major General Guingand, quoted in Flower and Reeves 1960: 461.
13. Churchill 1989: 629.

14. Montgomery 1958: 139.
15. NA, WO 169/5881, 3 December 1943.
16. Montgomery 1958: 148.
17. NA, WO 169/5881, 25 December 1943.
18. Letter to *The Times* from the president of the fund (Livesey 1989: 176–7).

4. Last Race in the Benghazi Handicap

1. Playfair and Molony 1966: 233.
2. Jackson 1975: 38–9.
3. Thwaite 1969: 29.
4. NA, WO 169/11587.
5. Bourke 2001: 126.
6. Sprawson 1992: 6.
7. Montgomery 1958: 163.
8. Villard 1956: 112.
9. Conversation with Bill's son-in-law, Barrie Selwyn, July 2006.
10. Thwaite 1969: 143–4.
11. Molony 1973: 21.
12. Churchill 1989: 661.
13. Ibid.: 662.
14. NA, WO 169/11587.
15. Molony 1973: 30.
16. Villard 1956: 86.

5. An Orchard in Sunny Sicily

1. A speech by Mussolini made in Palermo and quoted in Follain, 2005 (frontispiece).
2. Hoyt 2002: 16.
3. Molony 1973: 42.
4. Ibid.: 99–100.
5. Ibid.: 60.
6. NA, WO 169/11587, 24 July 1943.
7. NA, WO 169/11587, 24 and 25 July 1943.
8. Flower and Reeves 1960: 635.
9. Molony 1973: 11.
10. NA, WO 169/11587, 15 August 1943.
11. Follain 2005: 306.

12.   Ibid.: 258.
13.   Bent 1953: 8.
14.   Hoggart 1990: 50.
15.   Bent 1953: 109.
16.   In the South African Army, basic pay in 1943 for 'coloureds' was half that of whites, and blacks got two-thirds of the rate for coloureds (Somerville 1998: 187–9).
17.   Bent 1953: 51.
18.   NA, WO 169/11587, 22 September 1943.
19.   NA, WO 169/11587, 26 September 1943.
20.   A 'gib' usually means a gaol but, according to the OED, 'to gib' can mean to disembowel and the description suggests that George does mean a loo.
21.   Follain. 2005: 264.
22.   Baedeker 1930: 431 et seq.
23.   The observatory was destroyed in an eruption in 1971, and the Cantoniera was destroyed in 1983 but rebuilt in 1985.
24.   NA, WO 169/11588, 12 November 1943.
25.   NA, WO 169/11587, 15–17 December 1943.
26.   NA, WO 169/11587, 25 December 1943.
27.   Kilgarriff 1998: 110.
28.   NA, WO 170/2291.
29.   Quoted in Trevelyan 1981: 144.
30.   Taylor 1965: 575–6.

6. The San Carlo Opera Company Is Still Singing

1.   NA, WO 170/2291, 2 and 3 February 1944.
2.   NA, WO 170/2291, 11 and 26 February 1944.
3.   NA, WO 170/2291, 19 April and 8 June 1944.
4.   Trevelyan 1981: 36–7.
5.   Lewis 1978: 101.
6.   Ibid.: 86.
7.   Hoggart 1990: 49.
8.   Lewis 1978: 46.
9.   Ibid.: 74–5.
10.   Bourke 2001: 170.
11.   Taylor 1965: 583.
12.   Trevelyan 1981: 303.

13.　The civilian labour was paid £2,132 for the period of 1–15 June, and by 16 June there were 222 male and 614 female labourers (NA, WO 170/2291 16 and 31 June 1944).

14.　NA, WO 170/2291, 7 June 1944.

15.　Slonimsky 1988: 540.

16.　Weschler-Vered 1986: 115.

17.　Hoggart 1990: 52–3.

18　NA, WO 169/11587, 4 December 1943, and NA, WO 170/2291, 12 December 1944.

19.　NA, WO 170/2291.

7. Python Rears Its Head and Wriggles

1.　'Re-allocation of man-power between armed forces and civilian employment during any interim period between the defeat of Germany and the defeat of Japan', white paper, September 1944, Cmd 6548. The white paper stated that Class A personnel would be put on a reserve list for further military duty after eight weeks leave.

2.　Hawkins and Brimble 1947: 176.

3.　NA, WO 170/2291, 6 October 1944.

4.　NA, WO 170/2291, 15 and 17 October 1944.

5.　PRI – President of the Regimental Institute. It was a welfare fund.

6.　Churchill 1989: 829.

7.　NA, WO 170/2291, 25 December 1944.

8.　Taylor 1965: 479.

9.　In response to a specific question as to whether soldiers in the Eighth Army who had served 3½ years overseas were precluded from home leave until they had finished 4½ years, Sir James replied, 'The detailed conditions for leave, as distinct from repatriation, to this country are left to the Commanders-in-Chief overseas.' Hansard, House of Commons, 23 January 1945, col. 663.

10.　NA, WO 170/2291, 8 December 1944.

11.　Garfield 2005: 50-1.

12.　Hansard, House of Commons, 3 October 1944, col. 736.

13.　NA, WO 170/6103, 14 February 1945.

14.　Taylor 1965: 594.

8. On the Dole in Castellammare

1.   NA, WO 170/6103.
2.   NA, WO 170/6103, 15 May 1945.
3.   BLA – the British Land Army, which fought in Northern Europe.
4.   Hansard, House of Commons, 8 June 1945, col 1289–91.
5.   From Sir Kenneth Clark's obituary of W. W. Williams, quoted in Williams 2000: 87.
6.   Hoggart 1990: 61.
7.   Wayper 2004: 235–6.
8.   Hoggart 1990: 62.
9.   Wayper 2004: 173.
10. Hoggart 1990: 62.
11. By 1944, 'Large increases in allowances were made – a private's wife with two children now received 60s instead of 43s. By this stage in the war the serviceman was pretty well-off compared with his civilian counterpart.' (Hancock and Gowing 1949: 505-6.) In 1943 average earnings for a man was about £5 12s, for a woman £2 14s (Nicholson 1943, 5: 2).
12. Baedeker 1930: 173.
13. Bourke 2001: 177.
14. CMP – Corps Military Police, later renamed Royal Military Police.
15. CB – Confined to Barracks.

Coda

1.   Bourke 2001: 190–3.

Bibliography

Aspden, J. C., *A Municipal History of Eastbourne 1938–1974* (Eastbourne Borough Council, 1978).

Baedeker, K., *Egypt and the Sudan: Handbook for Travellers* (Leipzig: Baedeker, 1929).

Baedeker, K., *Southern Italy and Sicily* (London: Allen & Unwin, 1930).

Bent, R. A. R., *Ten Thousand Men of Africa: The Story of the Bechuanaland Pioneers and Gunners 1941–1946* (London: HMSO, 1953).

Bourke, J., *The Second World War: A People's History* (Oxford University Press, 2001).

Calder, A., *The People's War: Britain 1939–1945* (London: Jonathan Cape, 1969).

Churchill, W. S., *The Second World War: Abridged Edition* (Harmondsworth, Penguin, 1989).

Flower, D. and Reeves, J. (ed.), *The War 1939–1945* (London: Cassell, 1960).

Follain, M., *Mussolini's Island: The Invasion of Italy through the Eyes of Those Who Witnessed the Campaign* (London: Hodder & Stoughton, 2005).

Forster, E. M., *Alexandria: A History and a Guide* (London: Michael Haag, 1982).

Gardiner, J., *The 1940s House* (Basingstoke and Oxford: Channel 4 Books, 2000).

Garfield, S., *Our Hidden Lives: The Remarkable Diaries of Postwar Britain* (London: Ebury Press, 2005).

Gooderson, I., *A Hard Way to Make a War: The Allied Campaign in Italy in the Second World War* (London: Conway, 2008).

Hancock, W. K. and Gowing, M. M., *British War Economy* (London: HMSO, 1949).

Hawkins, T. H. and Brimble, L. J. F., *Adult Education: The Record of the British Army* (London: Macmillan, 1947).

Hoggart, R., *A Sort of Clowning* (London: Chatto & Windus, 1990).

Hoyt, E. W., *Backwater War: The Allied Campaign in Italy 1943–1945* (Westport: Praeger, 2002).

Jackson, W. G. F., *The North African Campaign 1940–43* (London: Batsford, 1975).

Kilgarriff, M., *Grace, Beauty and Banjos* (London: Oberon Books, 1998).

Lewis, N., *Naples '44* (London: Collins, 1978).

Livesey, A. (ed.), *Are We at War? Letters to the Times 1939–1945* (London: Times Books, 1989).

Molony, C. J. C., *The Mediterranean and Middle East, Vol. V* (London: HMSO, 1973).

Montgomery of Alamein, *The Memoirs of Field-Marshal the Viscount Montgomery of Alamein* (London: Collins, 1958).

Moorhead, A., *The End in Africa* (Bath: Cedric Chivers, 1973).

Nicholson, J. L., 'Earnings of Work People in 1938 and 1943' in *Bulletin of Institute of Statistics Oxford* (1943).

Payton-Smith, D. J., *Oil: A Study of War-time Policy and Administration* (London: HMSO, 1971).

Playfair, I. S. O. and Molony, C. J. C., *The Mediterranean and Middle East, Vol IV* (London: HMSO, 1966).

RASC: The Story of the Royal Army Service Corps 1939–45 (London: Bell, 1955).

Sattin, A., *The Pharaoh's Shadow: Travels in Ancient and Modern Egypt* (London: Gollancz, 2000).

Slonimsky, N., *The Concise Biographical Dictionary of Composers and Musicians* (London: Simon & Schuster, 1988).

Somerville, C., *Our War: How the British Commonwealth Fought the Second World War* (London: Weidenfeld & Nicholson, 1998).

Sprawson, C., *Haunts of the Black Masseur: The Swimmer as Hero* (London: Jonathan Cape, 1992).

Stevens, L., *A Short History of Eastbourne* (Eastbourne Local History Society, 1987).

Taylor, A. J. P., *English History 1914–1945* (Oxford University Press, 1965).

Thwaite, A., *The Deserts of the Hesperides: An Experience of Libya* (London: Secker & Warburg, 1969).

Trevelyan, R. *Rome '44: The Battle for the Eternal City* (London: Secker & Warburg, 1981).

Villard, H. S., *Libya: The New Arab Kingdom of North Africa* (New York: Cornell University Press, 1956).

Wayper, L., *Mars and Minerva: A History of Army Education* (Winchester: RAEC Association, 2003).

Weschler-Vered, A., *Jascha Heifetz* (London: Robert Hale, 2004).

Whiting, C., *Poor Bloody Infantry* (London: Stanley Paul, 1987).

Williams, G., *Green Mountain: An Informal Guide to Cyrenaica and Its Jebel Akhdar* (London: Faber & Faber, 1963).

Williams, G. W. E., *Williams: Educator Extraordinary: A Memoir by Lady Gertrude Williams* (Penguin Collectors' Society, 2000).